The Unfinished History of the Indebted Nation-State

Jonathan Hall

The Unfinished History of the Indebted Nation-State

palgrave
macmillan

Jonathan Hall
Bakhtin Centre
Sheffield University
Sheffield, UK

ISBN 978-3-031-84001-2 ISBN 978-3-031-84002-9 (eBook)
https://doi.org/10.1007/978-3-031-84002-9

This Palgrave Macmillan imprint is published by the registered company Springer Nature Switzerland AG
The registered company address is: Gewerbestrasse 11, 6330 Cham, Switzerland

Preface

Mankind could be born free but is everywhere in debt

In the opening sentence of his *Social Contract* (1762), Jean-Jacques Rousseau declared "Mankind is born free and is everywhere in chains". Nearly a century later, Karl Marx and Friedrich Engels urged the workers of the world to unite, declaring "You have nothing to lose but your chains; you have a world to win" (*The Communist Manifesto*, 1848). But now, after two world wars, the workers of the world are still chained to the nation-states system which divides them and sets them against each other; so the still unresolved problem is how to "lose" those chains.

This book will argue that the so-called "system" of competitive nation-states is the *provisional* outcome of a historical process which is now entering its belated moment of crisis. Resolving that crisis requires the recognition that it has now become *both possible and necessary* to abolish the indebtedness which enabled the nation-state form to emerge from its early feudal origins in Europe. The opening chapter begins with that emergence because it was the starting point for the long, but still unfinished, global history of the system of indebted nation-states.

Sheffield, UK Jonathan Hall

Acknowledgments I would like to thank my old friends and colleagues Craig Brandist, Ackbar Abbas, Jeremy Tambling, and Tim Cowen for their critical observations and encouragement during the preparation of this book.

Contents

CHAPTER 1

The Pre-capitalist Double-Bind and Its Persistence

Abstract This chapter argues that the endemic indebtedness of the nation-state, which has now become global, is the outcome of a *longue durée* history which should be traced back to the particular circumstances of its emergence in Western Europe. Early European feudalism was characterised by the competitive conflicts between warlords for the possession of land, which was the main source of wealth and power. But each successful warlord was caught in a double-bind: in order to maintain and expand his power, he was compelled to alienate some of his land rights to his potential rivals. The process of the "monetisation of society", which depended on borrowing from the long-distance traders of the time, provided the only means of exit from that double-bind. But that solution laid the basis for the eventual subordination of the emergent territorial rulers of the nation-state to the international power of their creditors.

Keywords Feudalism · Territoriality · Parcellisation of sovereignty · Monetisation · Double-bind · Symbiotic relationship · Pre-capitalist expansion · Tax burdens · Slavery · Eurocentrism · Transnational trade · War finance · *Fiat* currency

J. Hall, *The Unfinished History of the Indebted Nation-State*, https://doi.org/10.1007/978-3-031-84002-9_1

The origins of the modern nation-state formation are far older than the global expansion of European capitalism in the eighteenth and nineteenth centuries. They also date back behind the legal terms of the Treaty of Westphalia (1648) which aimed to establish a lasting peace between the warring European states of the seventeenth-century. That legal recognition of *national* rights, instead of the dynastic rights enjoyed by a ruler and his blood descendants, was certainly an important innovation in Western forms of political power, but the historical origins of the territorial nation-state have to be sought earlier. After all, the principle of territoriality had already been established by the Pope's arbitrary geographical division of South America between the colonising powers, Portugal and Spain, in the late fifteenth century.[1] The nation-states "system" (a misnomer if ever there was one) is the outcome of a long process of expansion with global ramifications, marked by uneven distribution across very different territories, but this chapter will argue that its origins are traceable back to its emergence from the feudal "parcellisation of sovereignty" in Western Europe.

We have become familiar with Perry Anderson's characterisation of European feudalism as the "parcellisation of sovereignty". Anderson argued that the feudal mode of production in Europe became systemic under the Carolingian empire as it attempted to restore the Roman Empire on the basis of Christianity.[2] Within that ideological claim to universal jurisdiction, sovereignty was nonetheless "parcellised" in practice, because the land itself was divided between the different warring landowners. As Norbert Elias emphasised in Volume Two of his *Civilising Process, State Formation and Civilisation* [1939],[3] early European feudalism was characterised above all by endemic warfare between the landowners, and those warlords who fought each other to become landowners. Since the land was the principle source of wealth, it was also the material source of power and was therefore the goal of those seeking

[1] The Treaty of Tordesillas, 1494. In the nineteenth century, the purely geometrical division of Africa into the different areas of exploitation by the competing European imperialists followed the same territorial logic, but without the help of the Pope.

[2] Perry Anderson, *Passages from Antiquity to Feudalism*, Verso 1981, p. 137. I return to this in Chapter 2.

[3] Norbert Elias, *The Civilising Process*, volume 2 [1939] Oxford, Blackwell, 1982. Elias' translator uses the term "monetarisation"; in this book I have opted for the more widely accepted "monetisation".

to obtain, maintain, or extend that power for themselves and their descendants. The struggle for the ownership of the land, and of the peasants who made the land productive, even included the "universal" Church itself, although its continuity did not depend directly on any particular familial descent. This system of "parcellised" sovereignty was largely non-monetary and was based economically on the local "demesne" mode of production. But that apparently autarchic economic form contained an internal contradiction which amounted to a systemic double-bind confronting the land-owning ruling class. Although Elias does not call it a "double-bind", he explains the objective basis of the contradictory imperatives which confronted that ruling class:

> Whoever was once entrusted by the central lord with the functions of ruling in a particular area and was thus in effect the lord of this area, no longer depended on the central lord to sustain and protect himself and his dependents, at least as long as he was threatened by no stronger external foe. At the first opportunity, therefore, as soon as the central power showed the slightest sign of weakness, the local ruler or his descendants sought to demonstrate the right and ability to rule the district entrusted to them, and their independence of the central authority.[4]

Consequently, every ruler was caught in the following inescapable double-bind: 1) In order to retain the loyalty of his followers, each successful warlord was compelled to concede to them various forms of stewardship over his conquered land, along with the right to appropriate the wealth (the surplus value) created by its peasant labourers, initially in the form of products or labour services, and later in the various forms of monetary taxation; But 2) at the same time, each overlord had to limit as much as possible this unavoidable alienation of land rights to his "peers", because it constituted his main weakness. The paradoxical designation of the King as *primus inter pares* (first among equals) expresses perfectly his precarious situation. Those "equals" were also potential rivals. In England, somewhat exceptionally, William the Conqueror was able to limit the fissiparous nature of his new kingdom, by controlling the distribution of his conquered land to those dangerous "peers" from the outset. But even so, the King's central control was always subject to contestation. Elias observes that when his son (Henry 1st) dies heirless:

[4] Op. cit. 16–17.

> ...the disintegration of governmental power on the island immediately sets in. The feudal lords build castle upon castle, mint their own money, levy taxes from their own regions; in short, they take over all the powers that hitherto, in keeping with their superior strength, had been a monopoly of the Norman central rulers.[5]

Elias points to "their ability to mint their own money", so they did not rely exclusively on the direct extraction of goods and services. But his general argument is that the "monetisation of society" resolved the problem of the endemic warfare which perpetuated the feudal predicament identified by Perry Anderson as the "parcellisation of sovereignty". However, I would emphasise that Elias' "civilising process" of *monetisation* did not really resolve this feudal double-bind structure of contradictory imperatives. What actually happened was that the monarch's dependence on the always dubious loyalty of his peers was supplemented, and largely replaced, by the monetary support of the transnational merchants and traders. They were his social inferiors and his political subjects, but they became increasingly indispensable to the emergent political centres, and to their expansion as they competed against each other.

The Emergence of the Contradictory Symbiosis of Market and State

When the Normans (the *Nortmanni*) settled in their new realm of Normandy, they soon converted to Christianity and became feudal landowners. This was an important change, because they ceased to be the fearful seasonal maritime raiders from overseas who traded their plundered goods (including captured slaves) in the existing transnational markets, located in various places. In the period of Viking dominance (AD 800–1100) Dublin was the leading slave market in Western Europe. But when these traders and raiders became landowners like the other feudal lords, the source of their wealth also changed. It was now the land which they had conquered, and consequently the labour of the peasants who made that land productive for them. They therefore "protected" the latter against plundering raiders, and against the other feudal land-grabbers. Under the feudal mode of production centred on the lordly *demesne*, these settled conquerors no longer depended directly on selling

[5] Ibid., 121–122.

their plundered goods on the market. As they became rivals in the contest for land ownership, their market dependence did not disappear but underwent a major reversal. In order to strengthen themselves in this deadly rivalry which characterised the feudal system, each feudal lord was driven to borrow, and it was this necessity which gave rise to the process which Elias' work calls the "monetisation of society". Monetisation strengthened the centralising landowners against their feudal rivals. It also enabled them to expand their territorial holdings and to maintain standing armies, (and, in a later phase, the navies needed to project their expanding power overseas). At the same time, the expanding power of the centralising territorial state increased the influence of the creditors who financed it. This was a truly symbiotic relationship of mutual dependence, because the mercantile creditors were, in their turn, politically dependent on the state which they financed. They needed the state bureaucracies and their legal codifications, backed by force, to override the myriads of different local feudal rights and obligations.

The crucial point overlooked by Elias is that the political rulers were not only landowners; they were also borrowers who could only repay their war debts from the surplus value which they extracted from the labour of peasants on their land. In short, not only did the monetary power of the transnational creditors finance the emergent European nation-states, enabling them to transcend their feudal situation and lay the basis for the possibility of political absolutism (never absolutely realised), but it also indebted the rulers of those emergent states, thereby laying the historical basis for a future control over them. In the early stages of European nation-state formation, the potential dominance of the creditors was not yet politically realisable. That is to say, the dependence of the emergent central rulers on their creditors was not yet a threat to their power. But as they expanded their territory, along with the military and administrative apparatuses needed to hold and control it, their indebtedness increased. Throughout this development, the debts incurred by the ruling class of landowners were settled out of the wealth which they extracted by the various forms of serfdom or taxation from the labour of the politically subordinate peasants and artisans. Despite all its subsequent mutations, this founding symbiosis of the territorial nation-state and extra-territorial monetary power is still with us. Even with the global development of modern capitalism, the constant factor has remained the dependence of the supposedly "sovereign" nation-state on the international monetary power of the market. Moreover, that subordination of the nation-state to its extra-territorial creditors is still held in place by its perpetual and increasing levels of indebtedness (to which I will return).

The strong point informing Elias' historical argument is that the monetisation of the relatively non-monetised region of Western Europe enabled the nation-state form to emerge out of its interminable conflicts for the possession of land, because monetisation strengthened central power, both militarily and administratively. But Elias did not focus on the relative weakness of the emergent state in its symbiotic relationship with the transnational mercantile power which brought it into existence by financing it. The power of the market is not part of his account of the "civilising" effects of the state's monopoly of violence, which imposed "the King's peace" within the territory under his (and sometimes, her) control. The process of monetisation did indeed strengthen the new centralising monarchs against their feudal peers and rivals, as Elias maintains, but in doing so it also made them dependent on their creditors. *So the old feudal double-bind structure reappeared in a historically new guise.* The indebtedness of the political rulers of the state to the extraterritorial monetary power of the market was open enough then (and it still is) but in the long run it had to be disregarded, known but overlooked, by the emergent national ideology. This new ideology would eventually demand its subjects' loyalty to the "nation", defined by its territory, rather than to the particular monarch and his/her bloodline successors (although in formal terms this hereditary monarchism still persists, and is vigorously defended in some places). But in the modern capitalist world, if the subjects of the politically unified nation-state are to be kept loyal, they have to be prevented from recognising that it is not actually autonomous, "sovereign", or all-powerful (whether that power is experienced as a source of terror or of reassurance) but subordinate to the requirements of international capital. And yet, that subordination is an open secret. Those theories of ideology which emphasise the centrality of the state to the capitalist "order" have to overlook this point, because they unintentionally perpetuate the nation-state's ideological concealment of its constitutive indebtedness to the external power of international capital. In the next chapter I will examine the role of antisemitism in maintaining the ideological fiction of the unified nation, which Benedict Anderson has called the "imagined community".[6]

[6] Benedict Anderson, *Imagined Communities: Reflexions on the Origin and Spread of Nationalism*, Verso 1983.

Viewed retrospectively from our epoch of bourgeois rationality, the reliance of the early European monarchies on the sanctity of the ruler's bloodline may appear to us as a persistent archaic myth, but at the time of their emergence it was crucial to each ruler's claim to legitimacy, however much that claim was contested by others. The almost obsessive production of ancestral charts which traced patriarchal descent (sometimes unavoidably through female inheritors) were quasi-legal documents intended to demonstrate legitimate inheritance. These charts were all more or less contrived fictions, with unavoidable lacunae and mythical founders, but that only demonstrates how important they were to the dominant ideology of the time. The patriarchal bloodline underwrote legitimate land ownership, which was the main source of wealth and power, and of course patriarchal inheritance was recognised by all the contending parties as the necessary proof of legitimate kingship.

The objection could certainly be made that Elias overstates the positive "civilising process" at work in the centralisation of power around the development of court society which, in his argument, laid the basis for bourgeois civilisation in Western Europe. Elias analyses how domestic pacification within the new polity was achieved by transforming the rival warriors of feudalism, firstly into armed defenders and then into mere courtiers in the service of Princes and Kings. But his book does not examine how that violence was not simply overcome within the centralising states. It was transformed, rather, as it was subsumed into the rationalised larger scale warfare between the emergent nation-states themselves. Nonetheless he refers briefly to the dualism within the process of "*the establishment of increasingly large, internally pacified but externally belligerent units of integration* [my emphasis]".[7] Those increasingly large and externally belligerent units eventually became our modern nation-states.

Elias' point is extremely significant, but he does not pursue it. The internal pacification was indeed the obverse of the external belligerence between the emergent nation-states, but it did not just happen, and it was not always successful. Civil wars, often motivated by a religious challenge to, or defence of, the Roman centre coupled opportunistically with continuing dynastic disputes, are an obvious feature of early modern state formation in Europe. They explain why internal pacification had to be

[7] Elias op. cit. p. 64.

enforced by the powerful new security apparatuses, partly to ensure loyalty to the ideological unity of the state (whether religious or dynastic) but also to guarantee its strength in warfare against its rivals. In the sixteenth and seventeenth centuries, these two motivations were not separable. The classic examples are Walsingham's extremely efficient intelligence services under the Protestant Queen Elizabeth 1st of England and the equally efficient power of the Catholic Inquisition in Spain. Viewed retrospectively, it is rather difficult to call this process of internal pacification in support of both internal unity and external aggression "civilising", but it was undoubtedly a necessary aspect of the early modern European nation-state, and this demand for national unity is still with us. Elias does not focus on their external belligerence or their domestic coercion, because his book is concerned above all with exploring the history of the *psychological* repression involved in the social process of establishing domestic control through internal pacification. His main example was neither England nor Spain but the culture of polite self-restraint which was eventually imposed on the French court of Louis XIV after the suppression of the last revolt of the aristocratic warriors of the so-called *noblesse d'épée*, known as the *Fronde*.[8]

A Eurocentric History?

Seen from a global perspective, Elias' "monetisation of society" may appear to be limited by its Eurocentrism because in reality the process of monetisation was far older than the emergent European nation-states of the medieval period, and in that earlier epoch it extended across areas far beyond the European land mass. Many non-European societies were undoubtedly more monetised, and were in many ways more civilised than the conditions prevalent in the marginal, economically undeveloped North Western outback after the fall of the Roman Empire (even allowing

[8] Under the *ancien régime* this aristocratic self-distancing from its past rebellious independence was imitated further down the social hierarchy, as the bourgeois town aped the aristocratic court. The consequent abjection of the "lower" spontaneous drives within the developing bourgeois self is the major historical theme, explicitly borrowed from Elias, which runs through Stallybrass and White's *Politics and Poetics of Repression* (Cornell, 1986). In their opening page they acknowledge that "the writings of Mikhaïl Bakhtin, Norbert Elias, Mary Douglas, and Pierre Bourdieu have been a perpetual and special source of inspiration for us" (op. cit. ix).

for the ambiguities of "civilisation" observed by Walter Benjamin[9]). But it was in the backward "barbaric" regions on the periphery of global trade that the social preconditions for the later development of capitalism were laid. Moreover, *it was on that periphery that the contradictory symbiosis of the territorial state and the monetary power of international trade first emerged and subsequently became the basis of unparalleled imperialist expansion.* Elias' thesis on the monetisation which enabled the rulers in early modern Europe to transcend the endemic feudal warfare in order to establish the centralising state (doubled by its externalisation of acquisitive violence) is compatible with Anievas and Nisancoiglu's otherwise quite distinct internationalist perspective, although that is not immediately apparent. In their *How the West Came to Rule: the geopolitical origins of capitalism,*[10] they too argue for monetisation as a key factor, because in their argument warfare strengthened the power of the merchant class within the European state:

> [A] byproduct of European feudal war-making was ... an attendant rise in the political autonomy, power, and influence of merchants, with increasing degrees of representation in the decision-making structures of states".[11]

Consequently, it was the class engaged in global trade which, combined with the dependent and relatively weak territorial state on its margins, laid the basis for the *pre-capitalist* expansion of Western imperialism. They draw a crucial theoretical distinction between the *pre-capitalist* states in Western Europe and the more developed *non-capitalist* empires elsewhere:

> The key difference between the functioning and socio-political position of merchants in the feudal-absolutist – and later capitalist – states in Europe, and those within the tributary societies such as the Ottoman Empire, Mughal India and Imperial China, was therefore the *structural dependence* [original emphasis] of the former [European] states on merchants for war-financing and social reproduction, which gave the merchants a relatively

[9] "There is no document of civilisation that is not also a document of barbarism", Walter Benjamin, "Theses on the Philosophy of History VII", *Illuminations*, Fontana 1973, p258.

[10] Pluto Press, 2015.

[11] Alexander Anievas and Kerem Nisancioglu, op. cit. p256.

> strong position of social and juridical autonomy. In Europe, governments often provided merchants with considerable resources and state backing.[12]

In short, the new imperial centres arose at first on the Western margins, where it was the weakness of the state in relation to mercantile capital which actually enabled that monetary power to benefit from the subordinate state's capacity for rationally organised violence (thanks to monetisation), and to impose their conjoined dominance globally. This preponderance of merchant capital in Europe led in turn to the development of large naval and commercial vessels capable of out-gunning all rivals and of carrying merchandise on the Atlantic and Pacific routes, in order to bypass the Islamic powers' control of the Eastern Mediterranean and the sea-lanes around Africa.

Anievas and Nisancioglu point out that in the thirteenth century, the nomadic Mongolian Empire boosted overland trade between China and the West by imposing its own form of territorial peace (which these authors dub the "Pax Mongolica") in order to tax that trade. This was a conscious policy on the part of the rulers of that huge land empire, and it served to boost Venetian mercantile power in the eastern Mediterranean. But later there were other unintended consequences which turned out to be equally important for the global expansion of Western mercantile sea-borne power. The Mongolian military threat to China meant that the latter had to invest enormous resources to defending its territorial frontier (constructing and manning the Great Wall, for example) which effectively put an end to its naval explorations beyond the Indian Ocean. So that area was left open to the Europeans, initially the Portuguese who came to dominate the spice trade between Europe and Asia, and went on to found colonial settlements in Goa and Macao. A little later the global trade flows were enhanced by the Spanish "Galleon trade" (which they do not mention, but could have) which was centred on the new trade hub of Manila. Manila was a new Spanish colonial city and a key hub in the trade which brought silver from the mines in colonised Mexico to China in exchange for commodities like silk and porcelain for re-export to the growing European market. David Graeber points out that for some time before the establishment of the trans-Pacific route via Manila, much of the silver exported from Mexico did not actually go to Europe but was diverted to Canton to meet the huge Chinese demand for precious metal.

[12] Op. cit. p. 257.

The Chinese had no use for European products, except for the precious metals extracted from colonised Mexico and Peru, and the exchange for silk and porcelain was conducted in terms favourable to the traders. They benefited even more from that exchange than from the delivery of silver to Europe.[13]

It is well known that Spain's importation of plundered gold from Mexico, followed by the silver mined in Peru and Potosí (modern Bolivia) enriched the landed magnates back in Spain, as well as the bankers in Genoa, Antwerp, and elsewhere. The enrichment of the landed aristocracy in Spain precluded the full development of capitalism there, while the bankers became rich by extending enormous interest-bearing loans to the Hapsburg monarchy to finance its wars to protect and expand its "Holy Roman" Empire. The other European monarchies were similarly indebted to varying extents. This imperial need to repay the interest on their war loans intensified the tax burdens on the peasant and artisan producers and ruined the Spanish economy. But, despite the four defaults on the sovereign debt during the reign of Philip 11 (1556–1598), the bankers' loans to the Crown were very profitable because their losses were more than compensated by the returns over the longer term. Within Europe, however, the other beneficiaries were the Dutch Republic after its liberation from Hapsburg Spain, and England where the capitalist mode of production was beginning to develop. Anievas and Nisancioglu observe: "There was therefore something to Walter Raleigh's often-cited maxim that "whoever commands the sea commands the trade; whoever commands the trade of the world commands the riches of the world and consequently the world itself."[14] Their overall conclusion is that the transnational process of "uneven and combined development" (adapted from the well-known formulation by Leon Trotsky) cannot be separated from the international commercial forces which made the uneven development of capitalism in Europe possible. According to this thesis, without this international process of "combined and uneven development", the previously marginal and backward territorial powers of North-western Europe like Holland and in particular England, could not have become the new global imperial centres.

[13] David Graeber, *Debt: the first 5,000 years*, Melville House Publishing 2014, p. 312.

[14] Anievas and Nisancioglu, p. 258.

In his *Blood and Money: war, slavery, finance, and empire*, David McNally develops this thesis further. He cites a number of other historians to develop his own arguments on the inseparability of trading, plundering, and slavery in the ancient Mediterranean world and elsewhere. In every case, "money and military power were indissolubly linked".[15] He even points to "the symbiosis of money and state building" as early as Ptolomeic Egypt, although money in the form of coinage issued by the state was not yet a universal equivalent. In the ancient Mediterranean world, the historical shift from aristocratic raiding and plundering, whose proceeds were shared among the warriors themselves, to systemic warfare and its reliance on mercenaries, required the vast expansion of exchangeable metal coinage, like the celebrated Athenian owl. That is why all these ancient states could not have developed without the labour of slaves who mined the precious (price-bearing) metals which could be monetised. McNally demonstrates that there was a long history of monetisation, linked indissolubly to military power, trading, and enslavement, all of which preceded by two or three millennia their subsumption into the early modern capitalist world. That was the belated historical moment when they were expanded to an unprecedented extent. But English capitalism led the field:

> For a prolonged period, Dutch merchants led all of Europe in the noxious trade of buying and selling enslaved Africans, though England eventually surpassed them in this bloody business as well. But England ran rings around its European competitors in the development of slave-based *production* in the New World. Contrary to those formalisms that counterpose capitalism to slavery and bonded labour, the historical relation was just the opposite. The world's first full-fledged capitalist power was in fact the most massive trader and exploiter of enslaved labour.[16]

This historical conjuncture is very important for understanding the development of modern capitalism, and its persistent effects nowadays cannot and should not be ignored or set aside. But, for the argument which I am pursuing, the unprecedented factor which gave the early pre-capitalist mode of production its political dynamism, paradoxical though it may

[15] McNally, *Blood and Money*, Haymarket 2020, p. 72.

[16] McNally, *Blood and Money*, p. 116.

seem, was the permanent indebtedness of the ruling classes of the emergent European nation-states. This indebtedness was not just incurred to pay for the rulers' wasteful appetites for Eastern luxuries (which was not new). It was driven and exacerbated by the persistent need to borrow in order to finance the warfare which was, in turn, made necessary by the economic compulsion to compete for access to markets and for territory with rival states. The whole developmental process was fuelled by the indebtedness which was the cause of the drive to expand and conquer new sources of surplus value (often in the name of a "civilising mission" which was the imperialist counterpart to Elias' narrative of the domestic "civilising process"). This too has persisted into the modern world, even when direct territorial control may seem to be no longer necessary for the extraction of surplus value from the subject populations. Under the conditions of our contemporary imperialism, whether it is acknowledged or not, the political control which ensures the continuing flow of surplus value has been delegated to compliant local agents or appointed "rulers". But modern imperial states retain their capacity for organised violence, and frequently exercise it. It might seem that Elias' concept of the ***monetisation of society*** as a process is not only outdated but also Eurocentric, and therefore plain wrong. However, "Eurocentrism" as a term of criticism (and sometimes of accusation[17]) loses some of its force if the matter in hand is the need to account historically for the global imposition of European political and cultural forms onto the previously more civilised non-capitalist empires such as the Chinese, Mughal, Ottoman and others, where the tributary mode of extracting surplus value was the norm. These political and cultural forms imposed on others included the nation-state form and, above all, ***its market dependence***.[18]

[17] Anievas and Nisancioglu accuse the so-called "political Marxists", like Ellen Meiksins Wood, of Eurocentric bias, platonic idealism, and even cultural arrogance, for allegedly seeing the origin of capitalist dynamics in Europe alone (and especially rural England). See *How the West Came to Rule: the geopolitical origins of capitalism* Pluto 2015, pp. 28–36. Elsewhere in their valuable book they are more temperate in their assessment.

[18] In the epoch of capitalist imperialism, this market dependence was new in one respect. The capitalist mode of production dictated the need to capture export markets for the industrial production of the imperialist countries. One outstanding example of the political nature of this capture was the British colonisation of India, which required the destruction of the local producers of cotton goods in favour of the manufacturers of Manchester, even though the Indian manufacturers were often more efficient economically than their English "competitors". Another prominent example is the Opium War

David McNally notes a key paradox in the relative weakness of the emergent European states, despite their endemic warfare: "Ironically, this was to give the European states considerable advantages after 1450".[19] He describes this advantageous position as ironic because the European monarchies were actually weakened by their indebtedness. To grasp this irony means following his narrative which charts a dialectical reversal. In England under Henry V (1412–1422) over two thirds of the royal budget were spent on war costs and in the last 5 years of Elizabeth 1's reign (1598–1603) three quarters were directed to war. Similarly, the Hapsburg dynasty spent over 75% of its revenues on war debts, as did the French monarchy. McNally's point about the generalised indebtedness is worth quoting in full:

> Incapable of significantly expanding financial capabilities and resources, states across Europe confronted incessant fiscal catastrophes driven by mounting war costs. The result was an unending series of crisis measures – emergency borrowing, forced loans, debasements of the coinage, debt repudiations – that undermined the longer-term financial viability of the monarchies involved. Indeed, for two hundred years after 1485, most European states repeatedly struggled to finance permanent debts brought on by the costs of war. Even the Spanish Crown, recipient of 40 percent of all the New World silver plundered between 1503 and 1660, came away from its military campaigns deeply indebted.[20]

In England the same situation persisted up to the Civil War (1642–1651) but even the execution of the King did not itself resolve the indebtedness incurred by the monarchy. This leads McNally onto his key point:

> In this context, any state that could establish a stable system of war finance was thus sure to accrue an enormous advantage.[21]

The apparently insoluble problem of the permanent indebtedness of the European monarchies to pay for their wars was first resolved in

conducted against China, which was aimed at the *creation* of a market resisted by the Chinese state authorities, like the international drug market nowadays.

[19] Blood and Money, p. 94.

[20] Op. cit. p. 95.

[21] Ibid.

England by the way in which paper notes issued by the Bank of England came to replace the general reliance on metal coinage in the late seventeenth century. This replacement was contrived by John Locke and Isaac Newton, but even they did not fully envisage what McNally calls the "revolutionary" impact of their own monetary measures. After all, the use of paper notes in lieu of cash was not in itself new. Much earlier Marco Polo had caused amazement in Europe when he reported on its use in China, and the use of promissory notes to facilitate trade became a fairly widespread practice in Europe. McNally carefully explains the "revolutionary" impact of Locke's and Newton's innovation in impeccably Marxist terms, although it was a revolution from above. Firstly, there was the immediate problem which had to be resolved. Even as late as their governorship of the new Bank of England (which was a private corporation, not a state organ), coinage was made of precious metal whose exchange value depended on the amount of socially necessary labour embodied in it. This made coins subject to illegal clipping in order to appropriate a portion of that value, and it became a particularly acute problem when there was a large difference between the face value of the coin in question and the international exchange value of the metal which made it up. That is why Newton was a fierce defender of capital punishment for that offence, not only in theory but also in his own sleuthing practices to track down the culprits and have them hanged. It was the international exchange value of the national currency which had to be defended.

McNally elucidates the "revolutionary" solution as follows: the stored value inherent in the metal coins themselves had always been created by the *past* labour of the mineworkers, whereas the value inherent in the banknote arose from the promise (ultimately guaranteed by the state) of a *future* extraction of surplus value. McNally's term "futurality" is the key concept here because it denotes a mechanism for the permanent availability of credit. Under Newton's and Locke's guidance, the new Bank of England managed to persuade a large number of private investors (whose profits derived from trade, including the slave trade like Newton and Locke themselves) to buy the national debt caused by war expenditure, in exchange for the promise that the state would repay the agreed percentage on their investment under all circumstances. This had not been possible under the notoriously unreliable Stuart monarchy, but with the bourgeois Parliament firmly in control over the royal budget when the "Glorious Revolution" (1688) had restored the monarchy under William of Orange (but now under strict Parliamentary control), the investors could be assured that the state would not default on its debts. Now the contractual obligations to the merchant bankers would be honoured without fail by recourse to the national tax revenues. Not surprisingly, taxation rates were for a time higher in England than elsewhere in Europe, but the Bank of England's promissory notes could circulate as an effective currency "as good as gold". In the next step, they no longer had to be interest-bearing. They became paper *fiat* currency guaranteed by the authority of the state. Although the promise to repay in gold was retained against the possibility of systemic crisis, it was not usually required. The promise itself was usually sufficient. The circulation of paper pounds was not purely domestic but, as Locke and Newton had intended, the pound achieved primacy as an internationally accepted medium of credit, and it supported British imperial dominance until it was replaced by the US dollar in the mid-twentieth century.

I have compressed the full complexity of McNally's historical analysis here, because for my argument the key issue is the persistence of deferred indebtedness within the new system of "futurality", meaning the assurance based on the capitalist state's guarantee to its creditors that all liabilities will be paid out of future tax revenues). Indebtedness is not magically overcome by a universal Jubilee which would cancel all debts (the original meaning of a Jubilee). Rather, any final settlement of debts (their "redemption") is deferred indefinitely, that is to say, for as long as the capitalist system of unlimited expansion continues to be supported by the creditors' expectation of adequate returns on their loans to the nation-state.

CHAPTER 2

Nation-State Formation and Antisemitism: A History of Duplicity

Abstract This chapter argues that anti-semitism has long been a duplicitous ideology inseparable from the expansion of the Western nation-state. Key evidence is supplied by Perry Anderson's *Passages from Antiquity to Feudalism* and Abram Leon's *Jewish Question: a Marxist Interpretation*, composed in 1942–3 but not published until the 1950s, after the author's murder by the Nazis. Leon points out that the long-distance Jewish traders financed the feudal rulers until they were replaced by the larger "Christian" banks, which is when antisemitism became a systemic ideology put into practice as violent persecution and expulsion. This developed initially in Western Europe before moving eastwards in a pattern which accompanied the expansion of mercantile capitalism.

Keywords International market · Sovereignty · Feudal economy · Creditors · Christian bankers · Usury · Imagined community · Scapegoats · Destruction of communities

In the previous chapter I considered the origin of the European nation-state form. To summarise briefly: viewed from the standpoint of global history, that origin was rather exceptional. The consolidated territories which later became the nation-states, first arose out of the unplanned conjuncture of the "parcellised" sovereignty of European feudalism on

J. Hall, *The Unfinished History of the Indebted Nation-State*,
https://doi.org/10.1007/978-3-031-84002-9_2

the one hand, and the *monetisation* provided by international trade on the other. Under the conditions of early feudalism, territory could be won and even expanded by successful warlords, but it was only the extra-territorial power of money in the form of credit which enabled the embattled warlords and their descendants to hold onto their territorial gains, to resist their rival "peers", and to become established as Princes and Kings. However, that retention of political power came at the price of their indebtedness to their creditors. This was not the case in the more economically developed and civilised empires elsewhere, like Mughal India or Imperial China. Those imperial rulers were not dependent on their merchant classes to sustain and reproduce themselves. This difference is of crucial importance. Even before the West became capitalist, the unique dependence of its territorial rulers on the credit provided by the extra-territorial monetary power of the mercantile classes laid the basis for the strength, and eventual dominance, of Western imperialist expansion.

* * *

All class societies are by definition riven internally by the division between the ruling class and the dominated classes or other 'subaltern' groups based on caste, race, or gender. These latter forms of hierarchical oppression (and of occasional resistance) are far older historically than the capitalist form which created the modern working class and, in doing so, incorporated all the pre-existing social hierarchies, along with their various modes of appropriating surplus value (plunder, slavery, serfdom, wage labour etc.) into its own "modernising" competitive dynamic. But the key point for this book is that the *pre-capitalist* European state came into being as a contradictory symbiosis of the territorial order of feudal landed property and the "monetisation of society" (Norbert Elias). This symbiosis provided the social conditions out of which the capitalist mode of production eventually emerged and developed. The pre-capitalist European states were clearly not autonomous, since they were only constituted as states through the loans, and the consequent indebtedness incurred by their rulers. That indebtedness continues to be the case, and this is an important issue because it means that even from its earliest beginnings the nation-state-to-be was never a fully autonomous territorial entity. From the moment of its emergence out of the embattled situation of "parcellised sovereignty" (Perry Anderson), it was always dependent on the extra-territorial monetary power of the merchants who financed it, indebted it, and later benefitted from its violent imperial expansion. The continuing dependence of the modern capitalist nation-state on the international power of capital cannot be fully acknowledged (but nor can it be completely denied) because unequivocal acknowledgement of that dependence would put into question its proclaimed "national sovereignty".

The ideology which supports and justifies the modern nation-state is therefore not a stable internally unified system, despite the assertions of many theorists. It is a dynamic activity, endlessly engaged in a covert struggle to negate the reality of the subordination of the state to the monetary power which gave rise to it, and under which it is still condemned to exist. This ideological struggle is not only expressed in ideas or beliefs. It is also conducted through visual symbols, or other symbolic displays of power like royal or republican processions, military parades, mass rallies and so forth, which address the public as spectators or participants, or both. Through all these ideological modes of address which attempt to secure the loyalty of the subjects of the nation-state (in Althusser's terms, their *interpellation*), the reality of its constitutive dependence on the international power of capital is concealed as much as possible. Not only does capitalist ideology attempt to conceal the underlying class conflict, in order to protect the capitalist system from the critical attention of those who could overthrow it (as most Marxists argue), but it also needs to deny, or at least obfuscate, the constitutive contradiction between the proclaimed sovereignty of the nation-state and the economic constraints imposed on it by the international market. This contradictory symbiosis of the ruling "order" (or rather, disorder) is consistently overlooked, known but disregarded, even by many in the ruling classes themselves. But at times of crisis like the present moment, when the means of production themselves have become irreversibly transnational, the undeniable dependence of every nation-state on the imperatives of the increasingly integrated international market constantly undermines the necessary ideological myth of its territorial "sovereign" powers. At the same time, however, that necessary myth of the sovereignty of the nation-state is unwittingly torn apart by the self-proclaimed "realists" who uncritically defend the capitalist order as a simply given fact. A well-known example is the late Mrs Thatcher who proclaimed that "There Is No Alternative" to compliance with the demands of the market, which in practice means acquiescence to its international institutions like the World Bank and the International Monetary Fund. She was not being original, but was simply restating an accepted capitalist commonplace in her usual dogmatic style. Her contemporary epigones endlessly reiterate this contradictory combination of patriotic loyalty to the nation-state with unquestioning subservience to the international institutions of late capitalism. Whether that contradictory stance is better described as a conscious self-serving hypocrisy or as a sincere but blind conformity, is in most cases simply undecidable. The important issue is the constitutive contradiction in the capitalist order and its supporting ideology, not the extent to which this or that politician seems to have resolved its double-bind imperative, to his/her own satisfaction at least.

The History of a Contradictory Ideology

There is a *longue durée* history behind the emergence of the ideological myth of the autonomous or "sovereign" nation-state. It is a history which matches the history of capitalism, and its relationship to antisemitism outlined in Abram Leon's work *The Jewish Question*,[1] which has recently re-emerged as a classic work of reference. This remarkable book was completed by Leon in 1942 when he was a leading activist in the Trotskyist resistance in Belgium, until he was captured in 1944 and deported to his death in Auschwitz. Leon's *longue durée* exploration of Jewish history, and especially of the divergent histories of antisemitism in Western and Eastern Europe, were integral to his own intellectual break from the nationalist perspectives of the left-wing Zionism of his earlier career. His book is not only a work of remarkable scholarship conducted heroically under very difficult conditions. It was also integral to his political turn to the even more difficult and dangerous struggle for working class internationalism. When Leon criticised the Zionists for their "utopianism", he was clearly relying on Engels' distinction between "utopian and scientific socialism". He could not have predicted that Theodor Herzl's quite explicit colonial ambitions would actually succeed in their appeal to British colonialism for support, and that they would bear the terrible fruits of displacement or eradication for the populations of Palestine. In the light

[1] Abram, Leon *The Jewish Question: a Marxist perspective*, (1946), Pathfinder Press, New York, 1970.

of this historical development, his use of "utopianism" as a term of criticism is certainly unfortunate, but it is perfectly understandable that in the circumstances of 1942 in Nazi-occupied Europe, this ethnically based "utopianism" would have appeared to be merely empty.[2]

Leon's history throws considerable light on the pre-capitalist indebtedness of the emergent nation-state in Western Europe. He argues that at first the mediation between the landed aristocracy, as it emerged from its early warlordism, and the transnational monetary power which supported that emergence, was largely conducted by Jewish merchants and usurers (i.e. creditors). Under the feudal system, this was a symbiotic relationship marked by both mutual hostility and inter-dependence:

> The hostility of the classes that live from the land towards trade does not eliminate their dependence on the latter. The landowner hates and despises the merchant but he cannot get along without him.[3]

This general point informs the subtleties of his history of the Jewish communities and of their relationships with the other "peoples" or "nations", for which he is sometimes criticised by later commentators. One of the difficulties presented by Leon's historical argument is his use of the hybrid term "people class" for the Jewish community. Enzo Traverso, for example, criticises this concept for its allegedly inflexible transhistoricism and reductive economic determinism.[4] But Leon's term does not mean that within that community there were no internal class distinctions, such as the differences between artisans, labourers, traders, moneylenders, religious leaders etc. Far from it. It is rather that in their relations with the other communities, and especially with the ruling class

[2] At first, the Zionist proposal for colonial settlement in Palestine held very little attraction for the Jewish populations in Eastern Europe and Russia, who preferred to emigrate elsewhere whenever permitted. Its main support came from the British colonial authorities in Palestine, who were guided by the policy set by the Foreign Secretary Arthur Balfour. Despite his personal antisemitism, he saw Zionism as both a way of preventing Jewish emigration to Britain and as a means of sustaining Britain's violent colonial control over the Arab populations. The United States followed Balfour's policy, but with far greater military and economic support for its new client state.

[3] Leon, A. op. cit. p 72. The hostility of the new masters found expression in the Christian condemnation of the trade in money (for example, Saint Anselm, Saint Jerome and others).

[4] See his *The Jewish Question: History of a Marxist Debate*, Haymarket 2019, especially pp. 179–185.

of land-owners, the Jewish traders fulfilled a monetary role as lenders on credit. In the long run that external relationship gave them a prominent role, which tended to shape the community itself. This activity was sometimes even reserved to them legally. In fact, there were several occasions when Christians who lent money on credit were accused of engaging in "Jewish" practices. The motives for such accusations sometimes arose from inter-Christian sectarian conflicts and repressions, whose victims were not actually Jewish.[5] Some have preferred to describe the Jews as a "caste", rather than as a "class", within the largely static feudal system. But for Leon they were a people who were distinguished from the other peoples or "nations" by the economic role assigned to them within the overall structure of relationships with others. He does not set out to define Judaism or "Jewishness" trans-historically, like the Zionists or their antisemitic antagonists. Indeed, his whole approach is a resistance to that ahistorical essentialism. Instead, he traces the historical constraints (and the opportunities), under which the Jewish communities adapted themselves to the others and prospered, or failed to prosper.

A significant moment of opportunity was presented by the decline of trading relations within the collapsing slave-based economy of the Roman Empire. This decline was partly a result of the withdrawal of the Roman aristocracy from their city functions, and from the cities themselves to their country estates.[6] In Leon's analysis, the Emperor Constantine initiated a major reversal which a modern reader of Antonio Gramsci might identify as a revolution controlled from above:

> Christianity, at first the religion of the slaves and downtrodden, was rapidly transformed into an ideology of the ruling class of landed proprietors. It was Constantine the Great who laid the foundation for medieval serfdom.[7]

When Constantine raised the persecuted Jewish sect (Christians) to an exalted social level, he made their outlawed monotheist religion the official belief system of the Empire. In actual fact, the economic effects of this

[5] The Albigensian heretics were sometimes subjected to that accusation. Enzo Traverso quotes Leon Poliakov's view that "the role of the Christian usurers, the Lombards and the Cahorsins, was much more significant than that of the Jewish moneylenders", op. cit. p. 182.

[6] Anderson: *Passages from Antiquity to Feudalism*, Verso 1981, pp. 93–94.

[7] Leon, op. cit.

revolution from above were more drawn out than its political enactment and its ideological justification, by which I mean Constantine's "solar" vision of the Cross and his miraculous conversion to Christianity which seems to repeat the blinding light of the conversion of Saul to Paul on the road to Damascus.[8] But the political revolution in the imperial superstructure was not immediately accompanied by the emergence of the new feudal mode of production. The "foundation for medieval serfdom", and its basis in the *demesne* mode of production, only came into being after the very long period of conflict and warlordism known to some as the Dark Ages. Perry Anderson argues that the Church was "the indispensable bridge between two epochs, in a 'catastrophic', not cumulative passage between two modes of production".[9] He adds that this "catastrophic" transition involved an ideological concealment of "the new" within the attempted recreation of the old:

> With the Carolingian State, the history of feudalism proper begins. For this massive ideological and administrative effort to 'recreate' the Imperial System of the old world, in fact, by a typical inversion, *contained and dissembled the involuntary laying of the foundations of the new* [emphasis added]. It was in the Carolingian era that the decisive steps in the formation of feudalism were taken.[10]

In labelling this passage from the old to the new mode of production "catastrophic" rather than "cumulative", Anderson appears to suggest that the relatively rapid appearance of the political order of feudalism was a revolution in the political superstructure which had long been prepared by slower underlying shifts and changes and only later became consciously organised. Be that as it may, Abram Leon's argument is that even before this belated institutionalisation of the feudal mode of production, the Jewish traders who had not converted to the dominant religion of the Empire, actually prospered. Over a long period they were not persecuted,

[8] According to this Christian conversion narrative, Constantine was on his way to do battle with his imperial rival Maxentius, when he witnessed the image of the Cross in the sun, together with the prophetic message: *In hoc signo vinces* (In this sign you will conquer). This solar imagery later became very important for the Jesuit Order, and for the absolutist claims of the centralising European monarchs like the "Sun King" Louis XIV.

[9] *Passages from Antiquity to Feudalism*, Verso 1981, p. 137.

[10] Ibid.

or at least not as much as the other sects who became Christian "heretics". They prospered because the conditions presented by the breakdown of the old slave-supported estates into "parcellised" landed property, allowed them to flourish. They fulfilled a necessary economic function:

> The more economic decay deepened, all the more did the commercial role of the Jews grow in importance. In the Tenth Century, they constituted the sole economic link between Europe and Asia.[11]

So, even within the emergent feudal system which marginalised and sometimes condemned them for practicing "usury", they nonetheless prospered because they were needed, not only as international traders but also as the providers of credit to the landed aristocracy, and especially to the monarchs. Leon cites Marx's *Capital* volume 3, in order to distinguish this early phase of mercantile capital accumulation from the later phase of fully developed capitalism. He focuses on the function of the Jewish trader within the feudal economy:

> The accumulation of money in the hands of the Jews did not arise from a special mode of production, from capitalist production. Surplus value (or surplus product) came from feudal exploitation and the lords were obliged to yield a part of this surplus value to the Jews. Hence the antagonism between the Jews and feudalism, but hence likewise came the indestructible bond between them.[12]

Consequently, there was an unacknowledged matrix which held them together, despite their mutual hostility, namely their joint exploitation of "mother earth" (below), that is to say the peasant labourers who made the earth productive. But within this feudal symbiosis, the Jewish merchant necessarily remained politically subordinate to the landowner:

> As for the lord, so too for the Jew, feudalism was mother earth. If the lord needed the Jew, the Jew also had need of the lord. It is by reason of this social position that the Jews were nowhere able to rise to the role of a ruling class. In feudal economy, the role of a merchant class could only

[11] Leon op. cit. p. 73.

[12] Leon, op cit. p. 77.

> be a clearly subordinate one. Judaism could only remain a more or less tolerated cult.[13]

However, this situation could not last indefinitely. With the growing accumulation of mercantile capital in the hands of the non-Jewish merchants, the status of the Jewish traders as creditors to the monarchs, and to the landed nobility, underwent a catastrophic decline:

> It is only from the Twelfth Century on, parallel with the economic development of Western Europe, with the growth of cities and the formation of a native commercial and industrial class, that the condition of the Jews begins to worsen seriously, leading to their almost complete elimination from most of the Western countries. Persecutions of the Jew take on increasingly violent forms. As against this, in the backward countries of Eastern Europe, their condition continues to remain flourishing up to a fairly recent period.[14]

This uneven development of the Western and Eastern European territories remained extremely significant right into the twentieth century. Leon links the outbursts of extreme antisemitism to the growth of mercantile capitalism in the different European territories as it moved from England to France, then Spain, before moving eastwards. This progression was marked by the replacement of the small numbers of so-called "Royal Jews", who were the lenders to Kings and Princes, by the large Christian bankers (like the Fuggers, the Medicis, the Frescobaldis et al.). Since the former Jewish creditors had been legally defined as the "slaves" of the monarchs, they could be violently expropriated whenever it suited their Royal masters to settle their debts by direct and brutal means. In this early phase, therefore, personal indebtedness was not yet the systemic problem for the monarchs which it later became for their successors. I will return to this development of *systemic* indebtedness because it lasted into the modern nation-states system.

Under the feudal system, the Jewish creditors to the great often operated as tax collectors for the Kings and Princes. So they attracted popular anger as blood-suckers, thus providing an additional service as convenient scapegoats who shielded the main exploiters from popular discontent.

[13] Leon, ibid.

[14] Leon, op. cit. pp. 73–74.

Needless to say, Christian tropes and narratives were also mobilised to incite and to justify the acts of popular retribution and occasional redistribution. These tropes included the New Testament story of Christ casting the moneylenders out of the Temple and, above all, the figure of Judas Iscariot, the traitor who sold Christ for 30 pieces of silver. The OED confirms that one of the primary meanings of *retribution* was *redistribution* or, more broadly, repayment.[15] Sometimes the popular acts of violent redistribution/retribution favoured the interests of the indebted nobility who encouraged them, even against the interests of the monarchs who protected "their" Jews. But, with the progressive development of mercantile capital, the politically subordinate Jewish financiers and intermittent victims of aristocratic or royal violence were replaced by the larger Christian bankers who could not be conveniently expropriated, even by the monarchs. It was at this historical turning-point that the political dominance of the landowning class began to give way to the power of their new (Christian) creditors.

The case of England after the Norman conquest of 1066 illustrates this point. In 1070, William 1st had recourse to his Jewish traders in Rouen to finance the defence of his new kingdom, and especially for the large-scale investments required for building castles. But from 1272 the future Edward 1st borrowed from the Ricciardi of Lucca to finance the Ninth Crusade, after which they were integrated into the royal financial system. They were followed by the Frescobaldi of Florence (1294–1312), Antonio Persegno of Genoa, followed by the Florentine Bardi and Peruzzi (1315–1345). The debts incurred by the English crown were huge, but were often covered by granting the Italian merchants the right to collect tolls or dues on the wool trade etc. In order to circumvent the Church prohibition of usury, the records are often deliberately unclear, but the rates have been estimated to range between 15 and 150%, partly depending on the urgency of the need to raise money for warfare.[16] As a consequence of this shift in the sources of credit, the only resort left to the former creditors to the powerful landed magnates was that of petty

[15] The *Dictionnaire Robert* likewise confirms that the moral sense of *retribution* was secondary to the primary meaning of repayment.

[16] See Adrian Bell, Chris Brooks, and Tony Moore, *Middle Ages: Loans to the English Crown 1272–1345*, in *State Cash Resources and State Building in Europe thirteenth-eighteenth century*, eds, Béguin and Murphy, Open Edition Books, Institut de la gestion publique et du développement économique, Paris 2017.

usurer lending to the small peasant producers. That is how the myth of the "Jewish" bloodsucker lived on, and even intensified. Since it corresponded to the daily experience of the impoverished peasants and artisans, it supported their "common sense" (Gramsci) and provided an ideological cover for the growing power of large-scale capitalism right into the twentieth century. Even as late as the nineteenth century, in Germany for example, the concept of "Jewishness" (*Judentum*) was synonymous with trade and usury. Some commentators find it disquieting that Marx himself used the term in this sense in his early *Jewish Question*, but he did so in order to argue for the progressive assimilation which would complete the liberation of the Jews from this social fate. That is how he understood the anticipated elimination of "the Jew" as a distinct social category. It would be part of a general emancipation.[17]

Leon's argument on the role of the Jewish traders and creditors in the pre-capitalist economy is closely echoed by Jean-Paul Sartre in his *Réflexions sur la question juive* written shortly after the Second World War:

> If the medieval Church tolerated the Jews, when it could have enforced their assimilation or had them massacred, that was because they fulfilled a necessary economic role: being accursed, they conducted an accursed but indispensable trade; being unable to possess land or serve in the army, they worked in the money trade, which a Christian could not approach without contamination. So the original curse was soon doubled by an economic one, and the latter is above all the one which has lasted.[18]

Sartre's brief historical observation can be challenged for its overstatement of the exclusions imposed on Jews everywhere. But it is matched by Leon's more thorough and more nuanced history. For Leon too, the pre-capitalist order needed to maintain the separate, but legally subordinate

[17] Leon too had expected assimilation to eliminate the separate social category of "the Jew".

[18] *Si l'Eglise du moyen âge a toléré les juifs, alors qu'elle pouvait les assimiler de force ou les faire massacrer, c'est qu'ils remplissaient une function économique de première nécessité: maudits ils exerçaient un métier maudit mais indispensable; ne pouvant posséder les terres ni servir dans l'armée, ils pratiquaient le commerce de l'argent, qu'un chrétien ne pouvait aborder sans se souiller. Ainsi la malédiction originelle s'est redoublée bientôt d'une malédiction économique et c'est surtout cette dernière qui a persisté*, op. cit. Gallimard 1954, p. 82.

status of the money traders. It permitted neither their assimilation nor their extermination, until their replacement by the large merchant banks in Western Europe made either option a real possibility. Sartre is mainly concerned with showing that this structural duplicity, built on a religious taboo which forbade usury, was accompanied by duplicitous social accommodations. For him that structural duplicity persisted into the hypocrisy of the antisemitic discourse of his own times. His immediate targets were the surreptitious defenders of the recently dominant ideology of Vichy France, and his book is largely organised as a polemical dialogue with their underlying presuppositions.

Abram Leon's history of anti-Semitic ideology is very incisive even if it calls for occasional corrections and amendments.[19] But the presence or absence of actual Jews within society at any particular historical juncture is not the main issue. After all, that presence could always be invented or overstated when required. Such inventions were quite common in England, for example, when there were only a few Jews left after the expulsions of 1290 (until their readmission, and partial assimilation, under Oliver Cromwell). The enduring strength of antisemitism has little or nothing to do with the presence of actual Jews. It is partly a false memory syndrome inherited from earlier generations. But the persistence of this traditional anti-Semitic *ideology* into the modern epoch is sustained by its imaginary transformation of the real but abstract (impersonal) power of international capital into personal but concealed controllers who can be blamed for undermining the harmony of the "imagined community" (Benedict Anderson) of the nation state. The persistent strength of antisemitism depends on this imaginary personification to account for the invisible and impersonal power of capital. It is in its own perverse way a nostalgic desire for a return to personal power.

Market Versus State: The Contradiction Concealed by Capitalist Ideology

Instead of the familiar structural analyses of capitalist ideology, including Althusser's concept of the state's unchallengeable *interpellation* of its subjects, critical theory needs to grasp the historical origin of the contradictory symbiosis of the capitalist market and the territorial nation-state

[19] The key work here Traverso, Enzo, op. cit. pp 178–215, *et passim*.

which is its form of political rule. The key issue is that the capitalist nation-states system inherited this contradictory symbiosis from its feudal past. At times of crisis in this contradictory political order, the scapegoating of the "Jewish" money man supplies the ideological means to prevent the subjects of the "imagined community" of the nation-state from consciously recognising its real, historically constituted, contradiction. For the modern revolutionary subject, the conscious recognition of the power of capital offers the potential for envisaging an alternative future as a goal to be fought for, but for those subjects of the capitalist nation-state who remain effectively loyal to its established institutions, any recognition of its contradictory nature is a potential cause for anxiety and has to be overlooked, or in psychological terms, disavowed. The ideological production of "the Jew", the "rootless cosmopolitans", the "citizens of nowhere", or the *déracinés* of right wing thought in the 1920s and 1930s et al., provides the defenders of the nation-state with the saving illusion of the concealed enemy who can be held responsible for undermining its imagined harmony.

There can be a fierce joy in this collective restoration of the "imagined community" to its supposedly lost or threatened integrity. The production of the embodied scapegoat is not just reassuring. It is also gratifying because it restores the desired illusion of a community rescued from corruption or disappearance. The violence of this restoration of the community, whether it is realised in physical acts of aggression or not, is now clearly reappearing on the current political scene. The gratification afforded to the crowds at Donald Trump's rallies by their ritualised aggression against their imaginary scapegoats is unmistakeable. Their discontent with the civilisation which downgrades and humiliates them is transformed into the fierce pleasure of collective anger (mis)directed against the presumed outsiders who have infiltrated the national community and undermined it from within. The manipulative refocusing of the crowd's otherwise directionless discontent onto the apparent reality of the embodied scapegoat provides its members with the satisfaction of a justified revenge (a vindication) yet to come. Antisemitism may appear to be somewhat marginalised nowadays, or even outdated amidst the other more overt forms of racism like Islamophobia (especially in the US where the older antisemitism is held in check by the ruling class' reliance on Israeli dominance in the Middle East), but it is still operative, and its strengthened resurgence in Europe too should be expected as the current crisis in the international capitalist "order" intensifies.

The Paradoxical Nature of Antisemitism

The long-standing appeal of antisemitism and its historical recurrence needs to be understood. It is doubtless a form of racism, but it differs from other racisms in one important respect. Most forms of racism simply mystify perceptible racial differences in order to misrepresent them as signs of essential "racial" qualities. While antisemitism also essentialises racial difference, it has always relied on the paradox of the invisible presence of the mythical "Jew" *which it then proceeds to make visible* to its addressees. This contrived unmasking or revelation of a concealed malevolent presence is central to the mythical figure of the "Jew", who is invariably represented as both a universal abstract power (invisible but everywhere present) and simultaneously a sub-human incarnation of monstrous bodily appetites. This aggressive unmasking may take the form of a purely verbal assault, but sometimes it has relied on visual caricature, sometimes on the pseudo-science of detection and bodily measurements, and sometimes on the brutal enforcement of visibility (there is a long history of the yellow badge from the sixteenth century to Nazism). In short, most forms of racism rely on perceptible racial differences which are easily made to signify the characteristics of an outsider or alien invader. The specific appeal of antisemitism relies on evoking the anxiety of the paranoid who hates or fears the *invisible* enemy concealed within the deceptive appearances of everyday normality. That concealed malevolence is frequently compared to a disease. But that invisible presence (whether hated or feared) is not a simple delusion, because the abstract and impersonal power of capital is indeed present everywhere, and at times of social crisis it really does destroy existing communities. Even Trump's faithful enthusiasts are not simply deceived by an empty myth, and nor were the Fascists in the 1930s. In both scenarios, the highly theatricalised production of *embodied* scapegoats satisfies the desire of the crowds for the otherwise invisible monster to be revealed. This contrived but satisfying revelation protects the real abstraction, which is the power of capital, from being recognised as the cause of the destruction visited on many communities.

However, this real destruction of communities under capitalism is itself a historically changing phenomenon. In the earlier stages of capitalist development, the destruction of community life was brought about by the enclosures of common land and the separation of the peasants from the traditional means of life. The Marxist analysis of this destruction of communities as the precondition for the development of the capitalist mode of production is broadly accepted by non-Marxists too. But Marx and Engels also observed that under the relentlessly revolutionising development of the capitalist mode of production, nothing remains the same: "All that is solid melts into air", in their well-known words. So in our present conjuncture the real destruction of existing communities also takes a historically new form, which may appear paradoxical because it is produced by the *withdrawal* of capital investments from wherever the exploitation of the local working class has ceased to be profitable. As a consequence of the falling rate of profit, the capital investments which used to sustain the working class communities in order to exploit them, are shifted overseas and leave almost nothing but wastelands behind. These are the "rust belt" communities to be found everywhere in the former heartlands of capitalist production. That is why, in many regions of the West, the current crisis is often experienced, not as an intensification of the rate of exploitation by the identifiable and familiar exploiter (the "boss"), but rather as the withdrawal of a supporting presence engineered by the concealed but still malign enemies of the people.

Especially in the United States, the manipulative revelation that there is an enemy within (often identified as the controlling élite behind "the deep state") gives rise to a fury which is in its way intensely gratifying. This anger is gratifying because, instead of an inexplicable disappearance or "melting" of the previously "solid" and familiar social order, which leaves an empty spiritual and physical "wasteland" behind, there is a theatrically contrived revelation of a concealed flesh and blood enemy who can be confronted and dealt with. But the current conjuncture in the US is not historically unique in this respect. There is a broader *longue durée* history of this reactionary, and literally apocalyptic, desire to have the concealed enemies unveiled or revealed (unveiling or Revelation being the original meaning of the Apocalypse), in order to turn them into reassuringly visible targets. These could then be expelled or destroyed, so that the absent order can be restored. The early modern history of this reactionary restoration of lost integrity is the topic of the next chapter.

CHAPTER 3

Purification and Paranoia: The Legacy of Early Modern Ethnic Cleansing

Abstract This chapter examines the cultural aspect of the founding contradictory symbiosis of warlordism and monetary power as it reached is apogee under the Hapsburg (Holy Roman) Empire in the Iberian Peninsula. Its spectacular displays of the purifying extinction of evil and impurity in the public *autos da fe* (acts of faith) were symptoms of a social order which struggled to assert its religious unity by denying its undeniable dependence on the transnational monetary power which was undermining it from within.

Keywords Inquisition · Ethnic cleansing · Blood purity · Spectacle · Baroque culture · Collective paranoia · Uneven and combined development · Threat from below

The long history of the hidden alien presence, and of the corresponding paranoid compulsion to unveil it, can be traced back to the attempted purification of the newly unified Kingdoms of Spain (Castile and Aragon) in 1492. In that year, the triumphant Catholic Monarchs decreed that the Jewish and Moorish populations must convert to Christianity, or be expelled on pain of death if they returned. This violence by the unifying and purifying nation-state replaced the earlier *convivencia* or relative co-existence of the three communities (Jewish, Islamic, and Christian), which

J. Hall, *The Unfinished History of the Indebted Nation-State*, https://doi.org/10.1007/978-3-031-84002-9_3

had seen the progressive creation of the Toledo school of translators and its highly influential transmission of Greek, Latin, and Islamic learning to Western Europe. For a brief historical moment, this coexistence had given a major impetus to the development of the European Renaissance, but the reactionary Catholic Monarchs were largely successful in their attempt to put that anti-feudal process into reverse. The ineluctable paradox underlying this triumph of the landed aristocracy in Spain is that it was financed by the increasingly powerful international creditors who extended large loans to the monarchs. In his *History of the Spanish Inquisition*, Henry Kamen points out that the ethnic cleansing promulgated by this invigorated feudal reaction in Spain was intended to create a single purified Christian state, but it actually functioned, *socially and psychologically*, to produce a proliferation of concealed identities. These hidden aliens then had to be unveiled by those infamous specialists in detection and confession in their pursuit of ideological purity. But even more suspect than the Jews and the Muslims themselves, who before 1492 had openly identified themselves as such, were the large numbers of *conversos*, i.e. converts from Judaism or Islam and their descendants. Their social identity was ambiguous and was therefore even more suspect to the so-called Old Christians who often resented their successes.

From 1492 onwards, the relentless Inquisitorial unmasking, or revelation of the secret "Judaizers" and covert Muslims even caused some disquiet in the Church hierarchy itself. This was partly because conversion was supposed to be a voluntary spiritual act but also, more significantly perhaps, because the felt need to unveil them meant that the sacraments and public rituals had lost their efficacy and could no longer be trusted. Thanks to this early modern hermeneutics of suspicion, the previously unquestioned social identities came to be seen as worldly illusions, or even hypocritical (theatrical) appearances, masking an inner essence. Worse still, the key to the secret identities was displaced from the purely religious sphere to the inheritance of the body and blood, where it appeared to have a more reliable natural presence. This blood inheritance was not endorsed by the official doctrines of the Catholic Church, but it supported a great many of the denunciations received by the Holy Office and pursued by them. Moreover, the Inquisition did issue certificates testifying to the hereditary *pureza de sangre* (blood purity) of their bearers. In historical retrospect we can now see that this early modern transformation of openly recognised differences of beliefs and practices into secrets concealed within the body and blood had a dreadful future ahead of it. In the nineteenth century, this ideology was updated and secularised when it came to be supported by an ostensibly materialist biological science for which religious beliefs and conversions were totally irrelevant. Henry Kamen's analysis also makes it clear that within this mounting collective paranoia, which was produced by the purifying drive in support of Catholic universalism, even the persecutors themselves could feel genuinely persecuted by the invisible forces which they tried to control by forcing them into confession, so that they could then be destroyed in the purifying fires. He also identifies the first known historical instance of an alleged "international Jewish conspiracy". This innovation was the invention of the well-known seventeenth-century poet, Francisco de Quevedo, who was proud of his own Old Christian bloodline. He accused the Count Duke Olivares of collaborating with the Jewish elders exiled in Salonica, who were allegedly plotting to overturn and reverse the purifying expulsions of 1492.[1] There is a link here with the later Russian antisemitic *Protocols of the Elders of Sion*, but not necessarily a textual influence. Both were paranoid symptoms, produced to defend an established hierarchy as it protected itself against the threat of revolutionary change from within. In both cases, that threat was perceived from within the framework of the dominant ideology, as a breakdown of order and a possible return to primal Chaos. So the defensive response to the threat of change required the production of scapegoats, who could be expelled or destroyed in order to prevent the chaotic breakdown of the established order.

Monetisation Versus Feudalism

The increasing monetary power which provoked this reactionary violence in the still feudal kingdom, made a great leap forward in the years following the expulsions of 1492. Coincidentally or not, that was the same year when the commercial drive to outflank the Islamic powers' control of the spice routes to the East had persuaded the triumphant Catholic Monarchs to finance Columbus' exploration of a possible alternative Western route across the Atlantic to India and China. Following the usual pattern of development in Western Europe (discussed in Chapter 1), this economic venture depended on borrowing by the two feudal monarchs,

[1] Kamen, Henry 31.

Fernando of Aragón and Isabel of Castile, which in this instance was organised by the *converso* royal treasurer at the court of Aragón.[2] But, as Abram Leon notes, even before this imperial expansion overseas, the triumph of the unifying monarchs within Spain itself had been secured by borrowing:

> The Jews constituted a source of considerable revenue for the kings. For example, in Spain, it was Jewish financiers, the Ravia brothers, who made it possible for the Castilian kings [sic] to bring the war against the Moors to a successful conclusion. Other Jewish bankers supported the Spanish kings in their struggle against the nobility. A special fiscal organisation, constituted for the collection of Jewish taxes, functioned in several countries.[3]

On the following page he observes that this financial arrangement which supported the monarchies against the nobility also divided the monarchy against itself. That was because, like the other landed aristocrats, the monarch too was deeply indebted:

> [But] while the king, in his capacity as representative of the State, was interested in protecting the Jews, we must not forget that he was, at the same time, a great lord and consequently one of their great debtors.[4]

The global expansion of Spain's imperial power in competition with Portugal after the discovery and conquest of America, is well known. But the internal contradiction, produced by the rapid monetisation of the feudal Kingdom through the importation of plundered American gold (and later silver from Potosí) is also historically significant. It had repercussions which even its immediate beneficiaries, the monarchs and their feudal rivals alike, could not control. The most obvious of these repercussions within Spain itself was the rapid inflationary spiral which impoverished the peasantry, ruined the artisans, and undermined the rental income which supported the petty nobility (the *hidalguía*). This paradoxical impoverishment of the Kingdom amidst its riches was visible

[2] John Rose, *Karl Marx, Abram Leon, and the Jewish Question: a reappraisal*, International Socialism 119, 2008. Rose emphasises the large numbers and the pervasive influence of the *conversos* in Aragon and Castile.

[3] Leon, p. 156.

[4] Leon op. cit. p. 157.

everywhere, and was widely represented in the painting and the literature of the time. It also fed the rampant antisemitism, whose passionate demand for retribution was sated by the spectacular public *autos da fe* (acts of faith).

Fernand Braudel, the celebrated historian of the emergent system of global capitalism, very acutely observes the ideological blindness produced by this internal contradiction, *within the same imperial state*, between the new transformative power of mercantile capital on the one hand, and its threat to the established feudal order on the other:

> Under Philip 11, Spain is less and less able to perceive the contradictions which grow more serious nonetheless. She escapes from the real. While her subjects are in revolt *and her riches ruin her* [emphasis added], she locks herself away in her interior castle.[5]

The "interior castle" is almost certainly a reference to Saint Teresa of Avila's mystical *castillo interior*. But a more recent investigation of the ideology of Counter-Reformation Spain identifies a broader cultural pattern. In his work, *The Metaphysical Peninsula*, Fernando de la Flor shows that in Hapsburg Spain there was an obsession with the rational science of military fortifications (*poliorcética*) which gave rise to a flood of designs for impregnable castles, many with the distinctly metaphysical meaning of the need to resist the return of the Flood, the threatening Chaos, and the clouds of darkness portending national and universal collapse.[6] De la Flor's work shows that the familiar melancholy of Spanish Baroque culture verged on a recognizably modern collective paranoia. For Braudel, this ideological turn to inner spirituality was a collective symptom caused by the ruling class' blind refusal (or inability) to acknowledge the reality of the social and economic changes that were actually taking place:

> There is a sort of symbol in the fact that the Merchants' Exchange in Seville and the Escorial were designed by the same architect. On the one

[5] Braudel, Fernand, *L'Espagne sous Philippe II, Paris, Hachette 1955,* p. 50.

[6] F. de la Flor, *La Península metafísica: Arte, Literatura, y Pensamiento en la España de la Contrarreforma*, Biblioteca Nueva, Madrid 1999; for a further discussion of the oblique representations of the crisis, see his *Barroco: Representación e Ideología en el Mundo Hispánico 1580–1680),* Cátedra, Madrid 2002.

> hand, *the traffic of the global market* which was overturning the world. On the other, the geometrically closed palace, modeled on the Castilian countryside, a convent and a cemetery, a place of study and of prayer, from where *a political power struggled to hold back the march of time.*[emphases added][7]

The mere fact that the Seville Exchange (the *Casa Lonja de Mercaderes*) and the Escorial palace were designed by the same architect, (Juan de Herrera, commissioned by Philip II himself) might be considered fortuitous. But the constitutive symbiosis linking these contradictory institutional sources of social power, was not. Braudel's own rather Baroque "symbol" unites these contraries (market and state) in a culturally defining *paradox* which anticipates the modern world. A paradox is usually understood as a rhetorical figure of speech which unites contraries without resolution. But there can be historically produced (social) paradoxes whose resolution is being actively prevented. In this instance, the internal struggle between mercantile capitalism, bearing a potential future capable of overturning the established feudal order, and the reactive struggle within the same feudal state to *prevent* that threatening future by arresting the "march of time" (which it also fomented), defines the inward fissure in this culture of proliferating paradoxes which we now call "the Baroque". But this early modern culture of arrested development was not merely static. The Spanish ruling class' ostentatious displays of grandeur, and its expensive but futile wars to defend its Holy Roman Empire, were symptoms of its refusal (or its inability) to acknowledge the disappearance of its own feudal forms of power.

Antonio Maravall's *Culture of the Baroque* supports Fernand Braudel's insights into this crisis on the threshold of modernity. He points out that the social and political crisis besetting Spain cannot be separated from the developments elsewhere in Europe. That is why he provides a general formula for understanding this overall European culture of intensifying inner contradictions and Spain's doomed attempt to arrest its own national development within it:

> The crisis of the seventeenth century cannot be understood in Spain without bearing in mind the broad European framework in which it unfolded, although in Spain its effects would turn out to be irredeemable

[7] Maravall op. cit. 50–51.

> for centuries. *It was the spectacular and problematic breakdown of a society within which forces driving it towards change struggled with other, more powerful forces whose object was preservation* [emphasis added].Wherever the resistance to these changes was greater, although in no instance could things remain as they were, the elements of the new society were not permitted to develop and all the factors of immobility become privileged.[8]

There are two important points here. The first is that even in Spain itself the reactive resistance to change was not fully achievable in fact: "in no instance could things remain as they were". Despite themselves, the reactionary political forces seeking to preserve the feudal order were compelled to negotiate with the dangerous forces of change. This was unavoidable because those destructive forces included the monetary power which was fomenting and financing Spain's own imperial expansion. The second point is that within Maravall's "*broad European framework*", there were marked national differences within the single overall process which Marxists influenced by Leon Trotsky have called the "uneven and combined development" of the international system of capitalist nation-states.[9] Even the almost legendary economic stagnation of Spain under the Hapsburgs, in which "the factors of immobility become privileged", cannot be understood in terms of Spain's national isolation from the inter-state rivalry which was eventually won by others. The idea of Spanish exceptionalism cannot explain the economic stagnation which had set in even before Spain's imperial apogee during the so-called Golden Age of the late sixteenth and early seventeenth centuries. Trotsky's thesis on "uneven and combined development" was first advanced to criticize the purely stadial view of separate national developments, which was characteristic of the Second International and was defended by Plekhanov who argued that Russia would have to follow the same path as the other more advanced capitalist states in the West. But the historical process of "uneven and combined development" also calls into question the step-by-step version of autonomous national developments within Western Europe too. For a long time, Spain was considered to be locked into its feudal backwardness. Despite the modernizing attempts

[8] Maravall, 26.

[9] Anievas and Nisancioglu, in their *How the West Came to Rule: the geopolitical origins of capitalism* make effective use of this formula, first advanced by Leon Trotsky. They emphasise the external factors contributing to the rise of capitalism in Western Europe.

by the new "enlightened" Bourbon monarchy in the eighteenth century, it appeared to have been left untouched by the phase of bourgeois development: "Europe ends at the Pyrenees", as the unattributed cliché had it. In the nineteenth century, this notion of Spanish exceptionalism was sometimes given a positive Romantic gloss when contrasted with the triumphant bourgeois mediocrity which had overtaken the other European countries after 1815. But Maravall's argument is that, on the contrary, Imperial Spain in the Baroque period was not merely (or exotically) backward. It was a modern nation-state, but one which was fissured inwardly by the contradictory global development which far surpassed its national territorial borders.

Braudel's and Maravall's observations on the *modernity* of the reactionary struggle against the possibility of change in sixteenth and seventeenth century Spain, illuminate the historical role played by anti-Semitic violence in the doomed struggle of the feudal aristocracy to maintain its disappearing social dominance. Even though the landed magnates benefited materially as a class from the large-scale importation of plundered gold from the American colonies, they blamed the Jews for the monetary dissolution of the divinely sanctioned order. The imaginary transformation of the impersonal power of capital into personal embodied agents who can be blamed and expelled (or exterminated) is the mode of scapegoating specific to capitalism. In the sixteenth and seventeenth centuries, that invisible malignancy could be imagined in religious terms as a fleshly "incarnation" (the Evil Spirit made flesh) which threatened the integrity of the "imagined community" of the Christian state. But this is not as outdated as the religious terminology might suggest. For the modern anti-Semite too, that monstrous embodiment of power can be detected and compelled to emerge from behind the veil of its day-to-day invisibility; so it can then be expelled or destroyed in order to restore the mythical lost integrity of the imagined community.

There is a collective false memory syndrome behind this anti-Semitic violence. Sentimental nostalgia for a lost simplicity, and its recycled forms of kitsch, are central components of this would-be restorative violence, not only in Hitler's Germany (and Trump's America) but in all the other capitalist nation-states in our epoch of global crisis. But the recurrence of this ideological duplicity in the twentieth century was not a mere repetition (or yet another example of the Nietzschean "eternal return"), because by then antisemitism itself had also mutated in accordance with the historically new alignment and confrontation of social forces. To be clear: In Imperial Spain, the potential for a different future which threatened to undermine the feudal order, and was therefore prevented as much as possible by the dominant aristocracy, was a future for capitalism (as Braudel and Maravall argue). But in the twentieth century, in Spain and elsewhere, the dreaded future being prevented (repressed, as much as possible) was the new threat from below, i.e. from the working classes (industrial proletarians or landless peasantry), while the social order being defended against the threat of revolutionary change was the dominance of capitalism, which was now politically established. In defending its newly established but precarious political order, the capitalist class was supported by its former feudal antagonists, despite the latter's continuing aristocratic hostility and contempt for the bourgeoisie. Faced with the new threat from below, the two former antagonists settled their differences, and jointly resuscitated the old anti-Semitic struggle for the prevention of the alternative future. This alliance of former antagonists was essential to twentieth-century Fascism with its ideological cult of the "timeless" ancestral past. In sum, the old reactionary struggle against revolutionary change was indeed replayed in the mid-nineteenth and twentieth centuries, but in the new context the "spectre" which was "haunting Europe" and was being "exorcised" by the new "holy alliance" of capitalism and landed aristocracy (as Marx and Engels put it), was the threatening potential for a post-capitalist (socialist) future.

Conclusion

This chapter has not been solely concerned with the fate of the Jewish populations in the Christian West. That fate was terrible, but it is not simply attributable to the complex religious dogmas and controversies of European culture, and certainly not to racial or ethnic differences. My argument is above all concerned with the historical emergence and subsequent persistance of our fundamentally contradictory social order (or disorder), namely the politically unified nation-state in conjunction with its antithesis, the monetary power of the international market. This contradictory symbiosis first arose in the West, but as it became systemic, the nation-state itself was increasingly subordinated to the power of the international market which had brought it into being. However, in our culture of so-called "late capitalism" this foundational symbiosis has also undergone a further historical development. In the *Communist Manifesto* (1848) Marx and Engels wrote that "The executive of the modern state is nothing but a committee for managing the common affairs of the whole bourgeoisie". That statement retains its validity, but it is no longer sufficient to describe the state apparatus as the "executive committee" of the bourgeoisie, because that description implies a large measure of effective control (and self-control) on the part of that class. In the modern world of "late capitalism", however, the state apparatus has become a politically uncontrollable war machine driven by the capitalist economy's demand for endless market expansion. That inexorable demand drives each state apparatus into ceaseless competition against rival state apparatuses in pursuit of the ever receding goal of unchallenged monopoly which US planners call "full spectrum dominance". No modern nation-state can choose to resist that demand. So the nationalist ideology which affirms the autonomy of the nation-state (against all the evidence) actually functions to conceal each capitalist state's lack of control over the international financial power which sustains its competitive drive against others. This inherent political weakness includes even the dominant imperial state and its rivals, which is why the *ideology* of the nation-state still requires the monstrous figure of the "Jewish" controllers or other surrogate élites who can be held responsible for the uncontrollable disruption immanent to it. The reality, which is concealed by this fictive production of the supposed hidden controllers, is the foundational contradiction between the impersonal international ("rootless") power of capital and the territorial nation-state which continues to be its form of political rule.

CHAPTER 4

Imperial Legality *Versus* Its Adventuring Warlords

Abstract This chapter argues that the pre-capitalist imperial expansion into the American continent depended on the same symbiosis as the formation of the nation-states in Europe itself, i.e. the contradictory conjuncture of territorial warlordism and the monetary power of the transnational merchant classes. The former's indebtedness to the latter fuelled the dynamic expansion, which continued even as it was intensified under the development of the capitalist mode of production, initially in the "home" territories and later globally. However, in the "home" territories the underlying class contradiction was masked, at least partially, and its social effects were dampened by national consensus, whereas on the colonial frontiers it was open and went "naked" (Marx). But with the outcome of the first inter-imperial global war, when the losers were forced to bear the debts incurred by that war, the "naked" violence of colonial domination came "home". Then the mask of restraint (which Marx called "the profound hypocrisy of bourgeois civilisation") was discarded and the brutal reality emerged. This moment of revelation is the key to understanding the political nature of modern Fascism.

Keywords Conquest of America · *Conquistadores* · Legal bureaucracy · Enlightenment legality · Charismatic authority · Barbarism · War debts · Disintegration · Return of the repressed

J. Hall, *The Unfinished History of the Indebted Nation-State*,
https://doi.org/10.1007/978-3-031-84002-9_4

The early modern imperial expansion followed the same pattern as the formation of the nation-states outlined in Chapter 1. On the one hand the rulers were in debt to the international creditors who financed that expansion, and on the other hand they had to meet their obligations to the warriors who put that expansion into effect. In 1492 the Spanish Crown borrowed considerable sums in order to finance the Genoese Columbus' mercantile adventuring, which promised to open a new Atlantic trade route to India and China. The creditors' financial risk was covered by the Crown's legal claim to any riches or land which might be discovered by Columbus and his companions,—that is, even when that unspecified land had yet to be discovered, and was still a legal fiction. But later, when the Conquest of America became a real process, the Crown had to acknowledge its earlier guarantee of certain limited rights to the land which the *conquistadores* had won on its behalf. Those land rights granted access to a proportion of the fruits of its enslaved labour through the *encomienda* (entrustment) system, which had originally been developed during the Reconquest of the Iberian Peninsula from Islamic rule. Without the services of these "Christian" adventurers the American empire could not have come into being (like the unified Spanish kingdom itself),[1] and even after the initial series of conquests they were still needed to maintain the imperial order. For their part they were not slow to emphasise their "loyal" services to the Crown. But in the new imperial context, the old feudal problem of the Crown's dependence on its adventuring warriors re-emerged. If the land rights conceded to them were allowed to become hereditary, the Crown would face the possibility of losing control over the conquered land, and therefore over the monetary flows from the enslaved labour on which it depended, largely to pay its debts to the Genoese banks. On several occasions, the disputes between the distant master and his "loyal" servants were settled militarily in favour of the Crown and its creditors. But the new imperial dominance over its potential rivals had not only to be won militarily but constantly maintained by the huge, and costly, legal bureaucracy described with great insight by Roberto González Echevarría in his *Myth and Archive, a theory of Latin*

[1] The legendary warrior adventurer retrospectively glorified as *el Cid Campeador*, the Christian knight who unified the Kingdom, was actually a mercenary leader who fought for himself, and sometimes for the Moorish kings.

American Narrative.[2] I will return to the role of this bureaucratic class, because its struggle to maintain control continued even after the national "liberation" from the shackles of the Empire.

Caudillismo and Charismatic Authority

The potentially rebellious class of warrior adventurers became the *conquistadores*, who were both necessary to the colonial power of the Spanish emperor in his American territories, and a recurrent threat to it. And even after the military defeat of the colonial power, they continued to threaten the post-independence bourgeois regimes. This threat took the form known as *caudillismo* which, as Edwin Williams points out, was not a new phenomenon:

> The term itself originated during the Reconquest of the Iberian Peninsula from the Moors, when a *caudillo* was the chieftain of a warrior band who organised raids against the enemy and built up a base for himself, *from which he could bargain with the king for the grant of titles and land. This, in essence, was the mechanism by which America was conquered and settled by the Spanish and Portuguese* [emphasis added].[3]

He also observes that the authority of the *caudillo* was essentially charismatic. I will return to this shortly. Moreover, he points out a very significant historical repetition:

> The emergence of *caudillos* in the nineteenth century suggests that there had occurred a reversion to political conditions analogous to those in the sixteenth. For, as in the decades following the Conquest, politics in Latin America after independence were violent and extremely fluid, and the reason for this was the same – the absence of a stable state with the authority to regulate disputes between different interest groups.[4]

[2] Op. cit. Cambridge University Press 1990. In Echevarría's own *longue durée* history of Latin American literary narratives, these lawyers and bureaucrats had a lasting influence on the formation of Latin American ideology, which is registered and developed through its major literary works.

[3] Edwin Williamson, *History of Latin America*, Penguin, p. 238.

[4] Ibid.

With the defeat of the Spanish Empire, the legal structures which had maintained the precarious stability of its "civilisation" were taken over by the Latin American champions of the European Enlightenment and its city culture. But they were all confronted by the return of those earlier rivals, namely the rural *caudillos* who had been a constant threat to the old blood rights of the monarchy. Now they continued to threaten the bureaucratic state and its rule of law, which had been taken over from the monarchy by the new national bourgeoisie. An eminent example of this embattled ruling class was a celebrated writer who was also the President of Argentina, Domingo Faustino Sarmiento. Even though Sarmiento is not very well known in the English-speaking world, it is worth taking a close analytical look at his writing, because his response to the return of the charismatic authority exercised by the *caudillo* Facundo Quiroga, is marked by a very significant internal contradiction. My analysis is largely influenced by the Hispanist scholar Roberto González Echevarría, and I will make use of his insights, but Max Weber's theory of "charismatic authority" is equally useful as a starting point.

In his *Theory of Social and Economic Organisation*, Max Weber calls the form of authority based on blood inheritance "traditional", and he contrasts it with modern "bureaucratic" authority. Weber's formal contrast has its uses, but no hereditary state, however absolutist, could exist without its bureaucracy. More significantly, however, both of these forms of state power, hereditary and bureaucratic, were threatened by the always possible re-emergence of the earlier personal form of power exercised by the warrior leader (in this context, the *caudillo*). For Weber, this is *charismatic* authority, which depends solely on the act of recognition by the followers of the warrior (or religious) leader. It institutes his unstable transitory power. Weber describes this relationship between leader and followers as "communistic", and in his view it is necessarily unstable. This is where his anti-socialism shapes his argument, because he sees the emergence of *charismatic* authority as a regression to the primitive origin from which the two later stable forms of state authority had emerged.[5] President Sarmiento's horror, inspired by Facundo Quiroga, is very pertinent here because he sees the *caudillo* as the bearer of this primitive and unstable "barbaric" authority from the Argentine hinterland (the so-called *barbarie adentro*). But Echevarría notes that Sarmiento's horror

[5] Weber, 358–392.

was nonetheless doubled by his fascination, and even grudging empathy. I will argue that this divided response has a social origin, inherited from the internal contradiction of European imperial dominance.

A Social Unconscious Revealed by Novelistic Discourse

President Sarmiento's celebrated work first published in 1845, *Facundo: Civilisation and Barbarism in the Argentine Pampas*, deals with the return of this "barbarism" from the hinterland. But he acknowledges that the "barbarous" *caudillo* was not simply alien to the modern "civilisation" of the cities. In his historical analysis of the revolutionary wars of national liberation in the southern continental "cone" (Argentina, Uruguay, Peru, and Paraguay) Sarmiento certainly sees the *caudillo* Facundo Quiroga in those terms; but he also recognises other qualities in him, namely the enviable strengths of self-reliant individualism and the leadership qualities of a potential Napoleon, which he associates with the *gaucho* culture of the hinterland. He even admires the natural courage and vitality of this "tiger", despite his horror at the unbridled savagery through which he exercises his leadership.

Echevarría's assessment of Sarmiento's divided response to Facundo Quiroga as a combination of horrified revulsion and intense fascination is extremely illuminating in this respect. It is not a matter of deciding whether Sarmiento was objectively correct in his description of Quiroga as a representative of *gaucho* culture. According to Edwin Williamson, he was not:

> The fact is that neither Facundo Quiroga nor Rosas [the Argentine dictator and Sarmiento's adversary] were *gauchos*, they simply used them and other lower class groups to further their own ambitions. Sarmiento could well have argued that these reactionary *caudillos* had exploited the *gauchos* and perverted their values ...[6]

Be that as it may, Echevarría rightly emphasises that the real importance of Sarmiento's book lies in the divided response which Quiroga, like the Argentine *caudillo* Rosas, evoked in the author himself. Echevarría writes:

[6] Williamson, 291.

> It is with fascination and repulsion that Sarmiento approaches Facundo Quiroga, *like someone delving into the darker recesses of his or her own subconscious* [emphasis added]. The grandeur of the book is predicated on this antithetical origin, a cauldron of warring contraries in which author and protagonist embrace like Dioscuric twins, joined and separated by their correlative differences.[7]

This "antithetical origin" calls for critical attention, because Echevarría's recourse to psychological individualism distracts our attention from its source in the contradictory political culture which European imperialism had inherited from its feudal past. This is not the clear and undoubted contradiction between the European conquerors and the conquered native populations, but the concealed inner conflict between the indebted imperial centre and its potentially rebellious, but indispensable, subordinate agents. My focus here is admittedly Eurocentric but it is significant because the issue at stake is the persistence, even within the post-independence regimes, of the old inner contradiction (which I have called its "double bind") within European imperialism itself.[8] President Sarmiento, the cultivated *criollo* Buenos Aires intellectual and champion of Enlightenment legality, exemplifies this internal contradiction with unusual clarity. As a writer he is clear-sighted enough to be disturbed by his own recognition of a previously unnoticed (i.e. unconscious) connection between himself and the "barbarian" *gaucho*.

According to Sarmiento's theoretical analysis of the civil wars following the defeat of the Spanish empire, the *gaucho* is a pre-social being who instinctively hates the repressive European civilisation of the city, whether Monarchical or Republican. That is why he sees Facundo Quiroga as a charismatic *caudillo* who revolts against all civilisation and puts his hatred of it into his bloody acts of unrestrained power:

> The Argentinian revolutionary war was double: 1, the war of the cities, arising from within European culture, against the Spanish, in order to expand that culture further; 2, the war of the *caudillos* against the cities, in order to free themselves from all civil subjection, and to unleash their

[7] Echevarría, 99.

[8] See Chapter 1.

> own character and hatred against civilisation. The cities triumph over the Spanish, and the countryside over the cities.[9]

In the outbreak of the "war of the *caudillos*" against the European culture shared jointly by the national "patriots" like himself and their Royalist foes, Sarmiento detects the emergence of a "heterogeneous" force *hitherto unknown to society itself*. In his own words:

> This force which breaks away is heterogeneous; the society which enfolds it has not known of its existence until then, and the revolution only served to make it reveal itself and to develop.[10]

Here Sarmiento clearly defines this "heterogeneous force" as a social unconscious, which only emerges into consciousness through the national revolution, even though he does not use that psycho-social terminology and certainly views it negatively. Of course, he could not have read Freud's theories on our shared instinctive hatred of the civilisation which represses those instincts. Nor could he have read Max Weber on the threatening return of *charismatic* authority onto the political scene. It is rather that his European cultural formation is similar to theirs and, in this instance seems to anticipate them. He does not use the word "charisma", but his description of the *caudillo* as a combination of warrior leader and prophet, a Tamburlaine or a Mohammed (who are his explicitly chosen examples), closely matches Weber's definition of "charismatic" authority. In effect, Sarmiento shows a troubled insight into the normally concealed link between the *caudillo* and his own cultural inheritance with its commitment to bourgeois Enlightenment values. He even sees the cruelty and violence of the *caudillo* as a return of the repressed which threatens that culture itself from within. For him, Quiroga's primitivism represents a disturbing buried truth.

[9] Domingo Faustino Sarmiento, *Facundo: Civilización y Barbarie* [1845], Doubleday Colección Hispánica, New York 1961, p. 69, *my translation*.

[10] Ibid. p. 67.

The Imperial Sublime

Sarmiento's narrative opens with a very striking account, which then turns out to have been narrated by Facundo Quiroga himself (or so the author tells us). Facundo, speaking through Sarmiento's narration, recalls his formative experience of being tracked by a "tiger",[11] fleeing up a tree, and feeling in his very flesh the primal response of the hunted man to the hunting animal's roar. Sarmiento's novelised Facundo tells the reader that this experience was when he truly came to know fear. The interchangeability of hunter and hunted, man and beast, is clearly what Sarmiento intends the reader to recognise in Facundo Quiroga. But, somewhat less explicitly, he endorses the *caudillo's* self-presentation as a leader who has encountered fear in his own body and has overcome it. Echevarría's illuminating analysis of Sarmiento's language (pp. 120–125) is too long to be quoted in full, but a key point is his detection of the "sublime" in Sarmiento's writing:

> The tiger's roar establishes a communication with the gaucho's flesh that bypasses language….. Tiger and gaucho understand each other subliminally, that which is being communicated being itself sublime: terror and desire. This identification and communication between tiger and gaucho by means of a sublime language says much about the masterstory embedded in Sarmiento's book.[12]

This may appear to be overblown, but in support of Echevarría's interpretation, I would add that Sarmiento's reliance on the many popular anecdotes concerning Facundo's words and deeds reveals his own conflicted acknowledgement of the leadership qualities in a figure who could inspire such stories:

> The repertory of anecdotes which fill the memory of the peoples with regard to Quiroga is inexhaustible; his sayings, and his actions have a stamp of originality which gave him a certain oriental outlook, a tinge of Solomonic wisdom in the outlook of the masses [*la plebe*].[13]

[11] There are no tigers in Latin America, so this term is rather European and imperialist. Intriguingly, however, the jaguar or cougar was often represented with divine qualities in pre-Columbian religious artefacts.

[12] Echevarría, op. cit. p. 123.

[13] Sarmiento, 90.

After relating one such event, with certain biblical overtones, Sarmiento again concedes to Facundo Quiroga a certain brutal superiority which gives him a real charismatic authority in the original meaning of the term *charisma* as "a favour specially vouchsafed by God" (Oxford English Dictionary):

> There are hundreds of such deeds in the life of Quiroga, which show him to be a superior man, while forging a mysterious reputation for him among the vulgar who came to attribute supernatural powers to him.[14]

In this passage, Sarmiento invokes the widespread tales of Facundo's prowess among his followers because they show that he was a truly "superior man" (comparable to Nietzsche's *Übermensch*) whom he covertly admires despite his horror, even though at the same time he expresses an equally Nietzschean disdain for the herd (the vulgar *hombres groseros*) who were so impressed. But I would add here that this same recognition of the *caudillo*'s terrible charismatic authority, which Echevarría very acutely sees as a shock of self-encounter on Sarmiento's part, occurred throughout Europe in the following century.

The Return of the Social Repressed: A Moment of Truth

That moment could well be described as a return of the forgotten or repressed truth of European "civilisation", both from its feudal origins and from its imperial frontier regions, because that is where the brutal reality of capitalist rule continued to be more openly exercised, and still is. As Marx wrote:

> The profound hypocrisy and inherent barbarism of bourgeois civilisation lies unveiled before our eyes, turning from its home, where it assumes respectable forms, to the colonies, where it goes naked.[15]

[14] Ibid. 92.

[15] Karl Marx, "The Future Results of British Rule in India" in *Marx Engels, Collected Works* vol 12, Moscow, Progress Publishers 1975, p. 221.

Marx's "profound hypocrisy" is the normality of the appearances which he denounces for their concealment of the reality of bourgeois culture in its heartlands. The distance which in normal times separated the illusions of European "civilisation" from the reality of its "barbarism" was both geographical and ideological. In the nineteenth century, this "profound hypocrisy" was never completely untroubled, but it remained generally overlooked because, although imperial violence was known and could not be completely forgotten, the barbaric acts always occurred somewhere else, out of sight. But with the advent of Fascism in the mid-twentieth century, the respectably concealed truth of European imperial culture is no longer concealed but "goes naked" in the heartlands too. At the time of systemic crisis in the late 1920s, the apparently outdated archaic violence of the warlord (*caudillo*) re-emerged within Europe itself as the concealed truth of its imperial culture. A strikingly literal example of the breakdown of this geographical-cum-ideological distance occurred when the Spanish general Francisco Franco broke his oath of loyalty to the new bourgeois Republic and invaded Spain itself from colonised Morocco at the head of the Republic's own colonial forces. Significantly, after his bloodstained triumph he proclaimed himself *Caudillo de España*. Amid this triumphal archaism he was welcomed by traditional Royalists and by many in the bourgeois middle classes too, despite their horror, at least in some cases. It is insufficient to attribute this enthusiastic welcome to simple opportunism, even if that certainly played a role. The more disturbing point is that, like the other Fascist leaders in Europe, he was welcomed by considerable numbers who recognised in him the emergence of a reality, hitherto concealed by the rationalism of bourgeois ideology. It was now re-appearing on the domestic scene where it promised to rescue the bourgeoisie itself from the future which it feared. It is insufficient to denounce the lies propagated by all the Fascist leaders of the 1930s and 1940s. They did indeed lie, on an industrial scale, but they also enacted for their followers the negated (socially repressed) truth of the capitalist social order. The emergence of Fascism was a response to the pervasive anxiety which gripped the ruling classes and those still loyal to the ruling ideology. That anxiety arose when the delusion of orderly progress on the basis of endless capitalist expansion was shattered.

With the collapse of enlightened middle-class confidence in the progress of "European civilisation", partly because of the industrial savagery of the First World War but followed a decade later by the Wall

Street crash. When the hollowness of the hitherto unquestioned institutions had become only too apparent, all the old imaginary strongholds of legal authority and power turned out to be patently empty constructs. Even the sacred power of money was reduced to (or revealed as?) millions of empty signifiers. But for many, especially in the middle and upper classes, and not only in religious areas, the anxious desire to recover the lost protective order persisted amidst the chaotic breakdown. This was not a simple conservative desire for its continuation, because it was actually the breakdown which awakened their desire for its restoration. But this time the older form of nostalgia for the lost order shifted towards a more conscious reactionary demand for the violence previously overlooked or held in check by the norms of bourgeois "civilisation". With the collapse of those norms there was a welcome for the personal "charismatic" Leader who openly proclaimed his barbarism, and his capacity as Leader to replace the empty institutional laws, his right and ability to sweep aside with contempt all the empty norms of bourgeois "civilisation", and to assume personal command by saying like Sarmiento's Facundo "Yo lo mando" [I command it].[16] This charismatic figure became an object of intense fascination for the former conformist and civilised bourgeois subjects, despite their horror. For some, the horror even seems to have injected a certain thrill of the Romantic sublime, which was supported by the public spectacles modelled on Hollywood cinematography, and by certain cinematic works too, like Leni Rieffenstal's Nietzschean *Triumph of the Will*. None of this is outdated in the present moment.

With the return of the personal charismatic "Leadership principle", which in reality was far more theatrically and cinematically staged than the old official state ceremonies, the abstract and impersonal legal constraints imposed by the bureaucratic state were overthrown (selectively, to be sure) in order to be replaced by a modern simulacrum of charismatic authority, with its demand for personal loyalty instead of the emptiness of bureaucratic legality. Carl Schmitt's "decisionism" offered a sophisticated legal justification for this abandonment of empty forms under a "state of exception", in favour of the supposedly "authentic" Leader who could suspend bourgeois legality at will, and replace it with a demand for personal loyalty. The fascination experienced by those subjects who were captivated by this theatrical display of personal power marks the moment

[16] Ibid. 62.

of the "return of the repressed" (Freud) of bourgeois culture itself. The subjects captivated by this theatricality rediscovered in their own emotional response to it the repressed reality of bourgeois civilisation.

However deluded it may be, the recoil to charismatic rule permitted by a "state of exception", is still an ever-present possibility. The violence inherited by bourgeois civilisation from its feudal past has never been really absent, let alone overcome or transcended, but it has normally been exercised offstage, "on another scene" (to borrow Freud's terminology). That other scene has usually been on the colonial frontiers, but also on the domestic frontiers (as in detective fiction, for example) which separate the metropolitan culture of the untroubled middle class from the *Jungle of the Cities*. Bertolt Brecht clearly understood the geographical frontiers of his contemporary capitalism, especially the colonial frontiers like British India or Southeast Asia, as scenes of its normally concealed truth. Likewise, the criminal underworld was the scene where the concealed truth of bourgeois society could be displayed, as in *The Threepenny Opera*, making it an object to be critically assessed (and not comfortably consumed) by the audience. As Brecht's close collaborator Walter Benjamin wrote at the time of its re-emergence in modern Europe: "There is no document of civilisation that is not at the same time a document of barbarism".[17] This version of the cultural "barbarism within" is not unique to a specific location, like the steppes of Asia or the deserts of Africa which Sarmiento compares with the pampas of Argentina (the Latin American *barbarie adentro*). It is the normally unacknowledged truth at the heart of imperial expansion itself.

What remains to be clarified is the reason for the emergence of that hitherto unacknowledged reality. Why did it not simply remain unacknowledged or successfully overlooked (repressed) by the polite hypocrisy required by bourgeois ideology as in Marx's criticism of "the profound hypocrisy" of the old imperial centres? The answer to this question lies in the response of the losers in the inter-imperialist conflicts of the early twentieth century. Those losers were confronted by the loss of the possibility for future imperial expansion. In the case of the Spanish ruling class, the loss of Cuba and the Philippines in 1898 to the rising imperial power of the United States was the underlying cause of a whole series

[17] Walter Benjamin, "Theses on the Philosophy of History VII", *Illuminations*, Fontana 1973, p. 258.

of crises within the old imperial heartland itself. The so-called "Generation of '98″ responded mournfully to that loss. Its leading figure, Ortega y Gassét" wrote in his *España Invertebrada* [Invertebrate Spain] (1921) that these losses on the imperial periphery were the first stages of the disintegration of the nation-state itself, but he did not mention the material loss of plunder to the US.[18] In the case of Germany after the First World War, the Versailles Treaty imposed the compulsion to pay all its outstanding war debts while it also stripped that losing nation of its colonial possessions, making it clear that the only permitted expansion was to be allocated to the victorious imperialists, the United States, Britain, France, plus Holland and Belgium.[19] The war debts would therefore fall onto the population of the losing nations. But since the capitalist system demands expansion, the only possible outcomes were either the overthrow of capitalism (as in the promise offered briefly by the new USSR which repudiated all the Tsarist war debts), or the continued competitive expansion through external violence on the basis of the promised future proffered by the emergent Fascist ideologies. The ideological cults of a return to the rediscovered national pasts, supposedly still persisting beneath the deceptions of the degenerate present, were central to this perspective of a possible future expansion within the continuing capitalist order. Nineteenth century racist ideologies played a major role, but they were a symptom of the underlying crisis of indebtedness, not its real cause. Italian fascism sought its space for expansion in a recovered Roman empire in the Mediterranean, while Germany turned its attention back to Eastern Europe, Ukraine, and Russia. This ideological recoil to a reinvented national past also imposed itself on the emergent but fast developing capitalism in Japan, which was admitted to the victors' club and awarded the former German colony in China (Qingdao) while China was excluded. In the case of Japan, expansion demanded the capture, represented as an Asian recovery, of territories still under the alien control of British, American, French, and Dutch imperialism. The common feature was the persistence of capitalism's need for competitive expansion which is inseparable from its system of international nation states.

[18] Ortega y Gassét, *España Invertebrada* 1921.

[19] While it is true that Italy, where the word and the concept of Fascism was born, was technically on the winning side, the Versailles treaty did not allocate to it the imperial spoils which it expected.

CHAPTER 5

From the Retrospective Transition Debate to the Revolutionary Transitional Demand

Abstract This chapter opens with a positive assessment of the insights provided by the so-called "Political Marxists", and particularly their focus on the market-driven compulsion to compete. However, the idea that the capitalist order in general depends on the "separation of the economic and political spheres" (E M Wood) ignores their contradictory symbiosis, and the consequent indebtedness of the Western nation-states, which is the theme of this book. A similar inattention is to be found in Anievas and Nisancoiglu's important book on Western domination. However, the broader issue raised here is that although the academic debates over the transition from feudalism to capitalism have yielded many important insights, (despite the many disagreements), the transition beyond capitalism is often left in abeyance even by Marxist theorists, who might be expected to be concerned with that question above all. This chapter argues that a retrospective understanding of the historical formation of the indebted nation-state has become crucial, but it can only become useful if it serves as a step towards the formulation of a revolutionary transitional demand for the abolition of all interest-bearing debt.

Keywords Transition debate · Transitional demand · Political Marxism · Agrarian capitalism · Market compulsion · Labour productivity · Capitalist accumulation · "Separation of economic and political spheres" · *Rentier* capitalism · Financial dominance · Ideology ·

J. Hall, *The Unfinished History of the Indebted Nation-State*, https://doi.org/10.1007/978-3-031-84002-9_5

"National sovereignty" · National debt · Nationalism · International super-exploiters · *Praxis*

The previous chapters have emphasised the pre-capitalist nature of the early European nation-state and its persistence into the modern epoch at the global level. The early phase of territorial expansion in the West was driven by the conflicts between warlords seeking to establish and consolidate their power as landowners. But this constrained them to alienate some of their conquered land rights to their "peers" who were always potential rivals. This was in effect a systemic "double bind" which confronted each successful warrior who became a landowning ruler: in order to strengthen his power, he had to diminish his riches and power as a landowner. This "double bind" could only be overcome by borrowing, which led in the longer run to the endemic indebtedness of the territorial ruling class to the transnational trading class. Before the capitalist mode of production emerged, it was the transnational merchants and traders who provided the funds for the emergence of the European nation-state, and later for its imperial expansion. These transnational mercantile creditors reaped considerable benefits from their loans to the political rulers. That is to say, even when the early expansion of the European nation-state had not yet developed into overseas imperial conquest, it was already driven by the economic compulsions imposed by the indebtedness of its ruling class.

Ellen Meiksin Wood's account of the emergence of capitalism in her *Empire of Capital* and her *Origin of Capitalism: a longer view*,[1] is broadly compatible with the history of the nation-state outlined in this book, except for her inattention to the indebtedness of the nation-state, which is central to my argument. In the *Origin of Capitalism* she takes up the debate on the transition from feudalism to capitalism, which had been ongoing between Marxist historians since the 1950s with roots going back to the 1930s. Together with Robert Brenner she insisted on the revolutionary innovation introduced by the capitalist mode of production. That is hardly new or contentious. But her major point, which supports Robert Brenner's intervention into the so-called "transition debate", is

[1] Ellen Meiksin Wood, *Empire of Capital*, Verso 2003; *Origin of Capitalism: a longer view*, Monthly Review Press 1999 [reprinted by Verso 2017].

that the historical emergence of the capitalist mode of production should not be described as a progressive liberation of the forces of production from the social constraints imposed by feudalism. She argues forcefully that such a view, unfortunately shared by a number of fellow Marxists, is unwittingly ahistorical. It rests on the assumption that capitalist tendencies are universal (even natural to all human societies) and were merely prevented from "normal" development, by the shackles of feudalism. Her counter-argument is that, uniquely under capitalism, the market imposed a historically new form of compulsion, which is still in force:

> Material life and social reproduction in capitalism are universally mediated by the market, so that all individuals must in one way or another enter into market relations in order to gain access to the means of life. This unique system of market dependence means that the dictates of the capitalist market – its imperatives of competition, accumulation, profit-maximisation, and increasing labour-productivity – regulate not only all economic transactions but social relations in general. As relations among human beings are mediated by the process of commodity exchange, social relations among people appear as relations among things: the 'fetishism of commodities' in Marx's famous phrase.[2]

Wood's and Brenner's historical argument is that the capitalist mode of production first arose on the basis of the outcome of the class conflict between landlords and peasant producers at a specific time and place, which they identify as the initiating moment of agrarian capitalism in C16th and C17th England. In an essay on this so-called "Political Marxism" Paul Blackledge provides a useful account of this "unintended outcome to the class struggle in the English countryside" and its equally unintended impact:

> In France, serfdom was destroyed by the class struggle between peasants and lords, but the process went beyond that needed for the development of capitalism, leading instead to the establishment of widespread small peasant property. In Eastern Europe the peasants were defeated, leading to the reintroduction of serfdom. Only in England did conditions evolve that were optimal for the evolution of agrarian capitalism.[3]

[2] E.M. Wood, op. cit. p.7.

[3] Paul Blackledge, *Political Marxism*, in *Critical Companion to Contemporary Marxism*, Brill 2008, p. 273.

Like Brenner, Wood argues that "the concentration of English landholding meant that an unusually large proportion of land was worked not by peasant-proprietors but by tenants …".[4] Consequently, unlike the situation elsewhere (France is her main example) in England alone:

> The relatively weak extra-economic [political] powers of landlords meant that they depended less on their ability to squeeze more rents out of their tenants by direct coercive means than on their tenants' success in competitive production. Agrarian landlords in this arrangement had a strong incentive to encourage – and, wherever possible to compel – their tenants to find ways of reducing costs by increasing labour productivity.[5]

This coercive power of the market also operated directly on the tenants themselves:

> As for the tenants, they were increasingly subject not only to direct pressures from landlords but also to market imperatives that compelled them to enhance their productivity.[6]

This market-driven compulsion to increase productivity first arose in England but after taking hold there, it was imposed internationally in competition with the other existing modes of production, initially within Europe but later at a global level, through the expansion of imperialism. So, for example:

> England was at the outset less advanced in commerce and technology than its Dutch rival, but its further development, both its successes and failures, was shaped by a distinctive system of social property relations, which made both producers and appropriators irreducibly dependent on competitive production. These property relations would set in motion a relentless compulsion to compete, to produce cost-effectively, to maximise profit, to reinvest surpluses, and systematically to increase labour-productivity by improving the productive forces. With that compulsion came all the contradictions of capitalism.[7]

[4] E. M. Wood, op. cit. p. 99.

[5] Ibid. p. 100.

[6] Ibid.

[7] Ibid. p. 94.

This view, briefly sketched here, became known as "Political Marxism" by its critics and by some of its defenders (including Wood herself). But it is a somewhat confusing label because their basic argument is that with the development of the capitalist mode of production, the dominant pressure on the primary producers of wealth was no longer directly *political* coercion but the new unavoidable compulsion to produce for the market. Everything, including the basic necessities for survival, became a commodity produced for the market, and it was only by satisfying its demands that even the producers' basic needs could be met. Under this emergent capitalist system, the labour of the producers itself became a commodity for sale on the market.

Wood's and Brenner's analyses are in many respects a response to, and extension of, the arguments on the history of capitalism conducted by Marxist historians under the wary auspices of the British Communist Party. Although these discussions contain many valuable insights into the role of the merchants *within* the English (and later, British) state from the C16th to the C18th, there is little or no exploration of the indebtedness of the Crown to that extraterritorial form of power.[8] In the last chapter of *The Origin of Capitalism* (revised in 2017), Ellen Wood returns to the existence of the pre-capitalist form of European imperialism, which had informed the opening chapters of her earlier *Empire of Capital*, and in *The Origin* she continues to insist on the joint development of capitalism and the nation-state:

> It is certainly true that capitalism developed in the distinctive context of the early modern European state, which was not itself created by capitalism – or, to put it more precisely, capitalism developed in tandem with the process of state formation.[9]

However, her intended clarification of this conjoined process ("to put it more precisely") obscures her own point that the early formation of the European nation-states actually preceded the development of the capitalist

[8] See *Ideology, Absolutism, and the English Revolution: Debates of the British Communist Historians 1940–1956*, edited and introduced by David Parker, Lawrence and Wishart, London 2008. The charge that these "political Marxists" theorise "capitalism in one country" has serious implications because the absence of an international perspective could imply an uncritical acceptance of the orthodox Stalinist theory of "socialism in one country".

[9] E.M. Wood, op. cit. p. 169.

mode of production. But she continues to affirm the *joint* development of capitalism and state formation without clarifying the contradictory process of its historical emergence. For her argument, the main point is that capitalism introduced the "characteristic separation of the economic and the political spheres":

> Although capitalism did not give rise to the nation state, and the nation state did not give rise to capitalism [?], the social transformations that brought about capitalism, with its *characteristic separation of economic and political spheres*, were the same ones that brought the nation state *to maturity* (emphases added)[10]

There has been quite a lot of disagreement over her assertion of the uniqueness of British capitalism: "…it was British capitalism that produced an imperialism answering to the specific requirements of capitalist accumulation." She argues that the capitalist mode of production first arose in England, which has been contested by some Marxist thinkers, but her strongest point (and the main concern of the "political Marxists") was to establish the appearance of capitalism as a historically new point of departure:

> Above all, capitalism created new imperialist possibilities, by generating *economic* imperatives, the compulsions of the market, which could reach far beyond direct political dominion.[11]

There is much to agree with here, but her repeated insistence that the "separation of economic and political spheres" was the historical culmination of state formation under capitalism, which she calls its "maturity" (above), leaves a major problem unresolved. For my argument, that problem arises from her inattention to the indebtedness of the state, *both* under the pre-capitalist imperialism of Spain and Portugal *and* under the imperialist expansions under capitalism, led by Britain and Holland (and France?) in rivalry with each other and with others.[12] Her view that the

[10] Ibid. p. 171.

[11] Ibid. p. 175.

[12] This pre-capitalist imperialism should also include England, in view of the early colonisation of Ireland under Elizabeth 1st.

"separation of economic and political spheres" is "characteristic" of capitalism fails to mention the longstanding *mutual interdependence* of the indebted territorial nation-state and the economic power of the international market. This is the contradictory symbiosis (my term) which the international capitalist "order" inherited from the European transition from feudalism to capitalism.

Wood's omission of the indebtedness driving the emergence of the European nation-states system and its global expansion, is not hers alone. Her major critics, Anievas and Nisancioglu in their *How the West came to rule* likewise make no mention of the indebtedness of the nation-state, perhaps because it was unique to the marginal situation of feudal Europe and therefore does not seem to have played a role in the "geopolitical origins of capitalism", which is the subtitle of their very useful book. This oversight is particularly striking in their case because the indebtedness of the European feudal rulers to the international traders should definitely be understood as "intersocietal", which is their key term. For example, when they analyse the short-lived predominance of the Italian banking families in the thirteenth century, they emphasise the political *dependence* of those Italian creditors on the military power of their debtors, but they disregard the consequent indebtedness of those same feudal imperial powers to them:

> The Genoese heavily depended on the protection of the Iberian powers, most clearly evidenced in the *Estado da India*, for the facilitation of trade. In this manner they remained subordinate partners in an alliance with an otherwise pre-capitalist imperial formation. The end of Genoese financial dominance in Europe was very much marked by their inability to control decision making in this 'colonial alliance'.[13]

The political dependence of the Genoese proto-capitalists on the dominant feudal powers of the time is indisputable, and may indeed explain their failure to emerge as colonial powers in their own right. But the unexamined aspect of this symbiotic relationship of debtor to creditor is that the indebted Iberian monarchies were not really free to exercise any autonomous "decision making" control either. While it is true that they were free to default on their debts, and often did, in the longer run their

[13] Anievas and Nisancioglu, op. cit. p. 218.

debts simply had to be paid (and indeed were paid). As David Graeber observes:

> [What's more] even kings were not entirely free agents. Charles V was continually in debt, and when his son Philip II – his armies fighting on three different fronts at once – attempted the old medieval trick of defaulting, all his creditors, from the Genoese Bank of St. George to the German Fuggers and Welsers, closed ranks to insist that he would receive no further loans until he started honouring his commitments.[14]

Consequently, in order to meet the financial compulsion imposed on them by their international creditors, these imperial monarchs were driven to expand their colonial tributary possessions, while simultaneously increasing the various forms of taxation imposed on the artisans and peasant producers at home. Viewed from the point of view of the indebted imperial monarchies, that successful co-ordination on the part of their creditors might well have appeared as an "international conspiracy", but the conspirators in question were not the older Jewish creditors. Indeed, the internationally coordinated exercise of economic dominance by the "Christian" banks was a power which the earlier politically subordinate creditors could never have dreamed of, let alone achieved. Despite their "absolute" appearances, the early modern Iberian ruling class of aristocratic exploiters were not really masters in full control of their own political hierarchy. (And nor were their political rivals elsewhere in Europe, like France for example). The absolutist monarchs certainly benefitted from the credit extended by the international bankers located in Genoa and elsewhere, but only on the condition that their debts had to be paid. Moreover, the surplus value for the settlement of their debts to their international creditors was extracted from the labour of their colonised and domestic subjects alike.

The Persistence of Rentier Capitalism

Ellen Wood's analysis of the historical emergence of the capitalist mode of production in England takes as its point of departure the outcome of the struggle between peasants and landlords. For Robert Brenner

[14] *Debt: the first 5,000 years*, 2014, p. 320.

too, that decisive moment saw the emergence of an effective collaboration between the aristocratic landlords and those more fortunate tenants who became incipient capitalists. In this conjuncture, both landlord and tenant were subject to the demands of the market, and their wealth depended on their joint extraction of surplus value from the labour of the emergent capitalist's landless employees. There was, therefore, a three-way struggle between the aristocratic landowner (who extracted rent), the tenant capitalist-in-formation (who extracted surplus value from the process of production) and the landless proletarian who unwillingly provided the surplus value to both. Despite this collaboration between the rulers, the capitalist came to resent the aristocratic landowner's power which compelled him to yield a portion of his profits in the form of rent. There was an emergent bourgeois ideology here, which regarded the aristocrat's rental income as an unearned burden on production, while the capitalist's extraction of surplus value from the productive process was considered to be earned because of the risk involved in capitalist enterprise. But it was not long before these two distinct means of extracting surplus value tended to merge, as the landlords often became capitalists too, despite their earlier mutual hostility.

With the global expansion of the modern capitalist mode of production, capitalist investment in agriculture by no means disappears. On the contrary, thanks to imperial dominance capitalist agricultural production has been globalised and has given rise to the various forms of "banana republics" everywhere (led by the earlier plantation production of sugar, tea, coffee, rubber, and more recently, soya beans). Its terrible effects on the populations, and the land off which they used to live, have become all too familiar scenes of disaster. To this ruthless extraction of surplus value, mandated by international market forces, we have to add the destructive effects of industrial mining and fossil fuel extraction. But capitalist land ownership also enabled the production of buildings as commodities, either for sale or for rent. The sale of this so-called "real estate" usually requires credit, which is provided by capitalist institutions in the form of mortgage debts imposed on the purchaser, while the leasing of the property to tenants enables the capitalist owners to remain rent-collecting landowners in perpetuity, i.e. for as long as capitalism lasts. In Capital volume 3, Marx remarks that "poverty is a more fruitful source for house-rent than the mines of Potosí ever were for Spain". His main point is the combination of landlordism with capitalism:

> The tremendous power this gives landed property *when it is combined together with industrial capital in the same hands* [emphasis added] enables capital practically to exclude workers engaged in a struggle over wages from the very earth itself as their habitat. One section of society here demands a tribute from the other for the very right to live on earth, just as landed property in general involves the right of the proprietors to exploit the earth's surface, the bowels of the earth, the air and thereby the maintenance and development of life.[15]

So nowadays, when the extraction of surplus value through the process of production becomes insufficient (due to competition and the falling rate of profit), there is an intensified turn to investment in property for rent. The direct "political" extraction of surplus value is not at all outdated (*pace* Wood). It is hardly surprising, therefore, that modern international capitalism has entirely forgotten its earlier moralistic anti-feudal denunciations of unearned aristocratic rent. The hedonism of late capitalism, which encourages infinite consumption and therefore the infinite expansion of the market, can certainly be described by the moralist as unrestrained "greed", but moral denunciation which depends on the presumption of a free choice, is a theoretical blind alley. It is far more useful to explain it historically by referring to Wood's and Brenner's insistence on the market *compulsion* to compete in order to expand, since any failure to expand involves the risk of bankruptcy. Certainly, unrestrained appetite or "greed" may well be a real social effect, which is even ideologically encouraged as a new good, but the compulsion to expand or die is a systemic necessity usually normalised as "growth", and cannot be reduced to a matter of ethical choice. Nor is it the operation of an ahistorical law of evolutionary selection and "survival of the fittest", as its apologists often claim.

Ellen Wood's reliance on the "separation of the economic and political spheres" to define the capitalist order, instead of exploring their mutual but contradictory interdependence, is not just a historical oversight. It occludes the continuation of this *contradictory symbiosis* within the present global nation-states system. In the modern imperialist world order, the compulsions of the market do not really "reach far beyond

[15] Capital 3, pp. 908–9, quoted in Rob Sewell, "Parasitical landlordism and the Marxist theory of rent", *In Defence of Marxism* (2017), November 19th 2021.

direct political dominion" as she argues, because the international financial market actually depends on the exercise of "direct political dominion", or at least the threat to exercise it, through the military or police apparatus of the nation-state in order to enforce conformity with its demands.[16] In the last resort, those demands are reducible to a single demand, namely that the indebted nation-state must pay the interest on its debts or, in the case of the imperial hegemonic state, that it must enforce others to pay, while permitting the indefinite deferral of payment by the hegemonic state itself (the privileged position enjoyed by Britain in the C19th, and by the US nowadays).

The Imperialist Paradox: Nationalism Supports International Capitalism

The early symbiosis of transnational creditors and debtor states was pre-capitalist, but this structure of state indebtedness persisted even as the imperial rivalry for territory and markets was intensified by the development of the capitalist mode of production. Moreover, the subordination of the nation-state to the financial market still persists under the conditions of advanced or "late capitalism" because the relationship of debtor to creditor, which is a contradictory symbiosis of mutual dependence, remains in force globally. This persistent structure retains the old pre-capitalist dependence of the political rulers on their creditors. In the modern world, all the nation-states, including the dominant imperialist powers, are dependent on the international banking system, and on the credit agencies such as the International Monetary Fund, the European Central Bank, or the currently hegemonic US Federal Reserve. But the latter international financial institutions are in their turn dependent on the indebted nation-states which are their creations. This dependence has two complementary aspects. Firstly, the international institutions depend *politically* on the nation-states' capacity to impose disciplinary violence when

[16] Ellen Wood's own formulation of this relationship is equivocal and ultimately evasive: "It will be argued in what follows that capitalism is unique in its capacity *to detach economic from extra-economic power*, and that this, among other things, implies that the economic power of capital *can reach far beyond the grasp of any existing, or conceivable, political and military power*. [But] At the same time, capital's economic power *cannot exist without the support of extra-economic force*, and extra-economic force is today, as before, primarily supplied by the state." (Empire of Capital, p. 5, emphases added).

the interest on the national debt has to be extracted from the population. Secondly, they depend *ideologically* on the necessary legal fiction of the "sovereign" autonomy of each state. This fiction of "national sovereignty" may be patently flimsy, and even demonstrably illusory in many cases, but it is nonetheless crucial to the whole international nation-states system, and it is ferociously defended. The illusion of national autonomy is necessary to the international system because only a "sovereign" nation can contract a debt and be made responsible for meeting the contractual promise to repay. That responsibility is usually known as respect for "the rule of law". Whenever there is a threat of default on the payment of the interest on the national debt, there is the all-too-familiar resort to direct coercion by the state apparatus in order to ensure the stability of the international financial "order" and the nation-state's continuing existence within it. That is to say, the nation-state has to act as a rent-collecting bailiff for international capital, even when the payment is to be extracted from its own population.

In sum, the "sovereign" state apparatus is required to put the direct coercion into effect (whether by violence or not, depending on the internal political situation) but the demand for that coercion proceeds from the international credit agencies, who are therefore the ultimate decision-making sources of power. No modern capitalist state apparatus can resist that demand, even if it wishes to (and mostly it does not). A recent example is provided by the acquiescence of the Greek government to the demands of the ECB and the IMF. But there have been many others. Latin America provides numerous examples (notably Argentina and Chile) where even the possibility of non-conformity with international debt obligations has been met by bloody repression conducted by the national state apparatuses. Nonetheless, the resort to state violence, or even the implicit threat of violence, has to be legitimised in the minds of as many of the subjects of the nation-state as possible because, apart from professional mercenaries and a few psychopaths, very few of its subjects would be willing to risk death, and kill many others, merely to defend the interests of international capital. That is the reality which cannot be stated bluntly, and has to be occluded as much as possible. Patriotic loyalty to the nation-state, whether sincere or feigned, plays a crucial (but paradoxical) ideological role in sustaining the international system for the extraction of surplus value from the subject populations.[17]

Nowadays, even within the dominant nation-states (including the hegemonic United States itself), the international financial institutions are actively impoverishing the working-class subjects of those territorial states by shifting their investments elsewhere, in pursuit of greater profitability for the owners of capital. This is a relatively new development. Even in recent memory, the European and American owners of capital used to draw a large part of their profits from exploiting the labour of their respective domestic working classes. Thanks to their imperial dominance and the profits squeezed from their colonial possessions, they were able to meet the demands of the domestic working class without undermining the profit system. In effect, under duress from the proletarian underdogs (through strikes, go-slows, and the threat of insurrection) they conceded some of their overseas profits to them. But in the current phase of global capitalism, market expansion in the face of the falling rate of profit has become unremitting in its demand that the investments in productive labour must be shifted to wherever labour is cheaper. In this situation, gains previously won by the working class at home must be reversed, whatever the political cost. Moreover, even in the non-productive sectors of the national economy, like the service industries (including health, education etc.) where the shift of capital overseas is not possible, the cost of domestic labour must be driven down in order to ensure its attractiveness for capital investment. Whether the holders of that capital are domestic or foreign is immaterial. What matters is that the working class, including the self-employed individual or even the small *petit bourgeois* enterprise, must be made to pay the interest on the national debt, whether through rising prices, raised interest rates, increased taxation of various sorts, or escalating mortgage and/or rental debts. Only the international hegemon is permitted to accumulate debts indefinitely, but here too there are constraints imposed by the international financial institutions. The current US national debt amounts to trillions of dollars. In order to reduce it and thereby maintain the value of US Treasury bills on the international markets, there has to be an increase in the extraction of surplus value, both overseas (wherever possible) and from the working

[17] As long as the nation-state system persists, there is indeed "no alternative" to this subordination, as Mrs Thatcher insisted (see Chapter 2).

population of the US itself.[18] This means that the market compulsion identified by Brenner and Wood continues to operate, even within the US where the national debt is exacerbated, as it always has been, by rising war debts to pay for past and present conflicts, or for the future conflicts which economic expansion makes unavoidable. In short, the political apparatus of the territorial nation-state, supported by the ideological myth of its "sovereign" autonomy, remains indispensable to the overriding demands of international capital. The new aspect of modern national indebtedness is the unprecedented expansion of political power in the hands of the armaments industries, whose products are marketed through the organisations of the nation state (like the Pentagon, to take the most outstanding example). As even President Eisenhower warned the American public (and the world), the power of "the military-industrial complex" is now the prominent example of this scarcely concealed, and apparently irresistible domination of the nation-state apparatus by private capital. But it is not alone.

The Transitional Demand: From Reformism to Revolution

In the Marxist terminology developed by Leon Trotsky, the transitional demand goes beyond the minimal demands which are labelled "reformist" because they can be accommodated within the existing capitalist order, however grudgingly, without complete disruption. In modern "advanced" capitalist societies, these minimal or "reformist" demands from below are usually formulated within the framework of established trade union structures (although reformist demands are sometimes made by a whole variety of progressive movements, which likewise do not necessarily challenge the existing system). Within the reformist perspectives of "trade union consciousness" the employers' resistance is always anticipated, but the usual aim of the union leaderships is to reach a compromise solution after a trial of strength (which is sometimes a token display)

[18] To some extent, this pressure to extract more from the working class within the US is increasing because of the international financial challenge from China. The latter rising industrial power is able to offer loans to the countries of the global South and elsewhere on more favourable terms (less debt burdens) than the US. However, it is unclear whether the holders of "Chinese capital" are necessarily Chinese companies or simply international lenders operating through Chinese political institutions.

followed by negotiation. The social democratic parties play a similar role, so long as the broad political consensus is not disrupted by underlying class conflict. This mediating role often carries material rewards for the bureaucratic leaderships because they serve to prevent any threatening political extension of the economic conflicts. In this respect, Ellen Wood's view that capitalism depends on "the separation of the economic and political spheres" is valid. But she does not state that this separation is maintained by the bureaucratic apparatuses, ultimately controlled by the state.

The *transitional* demand, by contrast, is consciously *transgressive* in the literal sense of the word: it knowingly "steps beyond" the established boundaries of the normal channels of negotiation. This means that it is oriented towards the revolutionary possibilities for a different future. Depending on the ideological points of view held by the contending parties, the transitional demand is either destructive and potentially criminal (a "transgression") because it threatens the existing order of things, or else it is potentially creative because it opens up the possibility of a new (socialist) order which can be brought into being by and for the working class. From the point of view of a revolutionary party, or a movement seeking to organise itself as such, the formulation of a transitional demand is crucial. It cannot be just the expression of a utopian ideal, however militant its critical language may be. There have been many perceptive analyses of the ways in which the working class is politically divided by race, gender, and/or nationality and is therefore subordinated to the interests of capital, but the problem is to find a way to connect such critical analyses (which may satisfy the theoretician) with the present experience, and the corresponding consciousness, of the exploited majority. Overcoming this gap is both a practical and theoretical task.

The debate over the transition from feudalism to capitalism, with which I began this chapter, stopped at analysing how the present situation arose out of the conflicts and occasional alliances of the past. But the transitional demand takes a step beyond this retrospective historicism because it proposes the measures required to transform the present situation into an *interim* phase in the struggle to create a future which will transcend it. This means that the present situation has to be understood, not as a historical endpoint but as the provisional outcome of the still ongoing conflicts inherited from the past. Only through such a historical awareness can the present experiences of the exploited enable them to reach a conscious understanding of *both the need and the possibility* of overcoming them in practice. This practical grasp informed by conscious understanding (in Gramsci's terms, a *praxis*) has to mean understanding the present experiences historically: that is to say, not only how and why they came into being but also, and above all, how they can be transformed (or sublated) into the basis for a future which will not merely repeat the past. For this reason a transitional demand has to be supported by a programme capable of winning the support of the exploited majority.

The analysis of the long history of the indebted nation-state system set out in this short book has been aimed at elucidating the current situation, in which increasingly large numbers of the subjects of the now globalised nation-states system are being crushed by unpayable debts, whether to the nation-state apparatus itself through the various forms of taxation, or to the privately owned investment organisations, such as mortgage companies, banks, or other lending agencies, legal or illegal. The ultimate beneficiaries of all these methods of extracting surplus value are the large-scale providers of international credit. They have become supremely powerful, but in practice the exercise of their power still depends on the political apparatuses of the nation-states. The latter are the enforcers of debt repayments when required, but they are themselves deeply indebted to their international creditors. Whenever a nation-state is on the point of bankruptcy, meaning that its debts cannot be paid, an international credit agency like the European Central Bank, the World Bank, or the International Monetary Fund always intervenes with a benevolently labelled "rescue package". Like the classical mafia offer, this package is an offer which cannot be refused. However it is beginning to dawn on the consciousness of many of the indebted populations that it is not they who are being rescued from collapse but the system of their exploitation. This dawning realisation does not guarantee the coming daylight, of course, but it introduces the possibility for its emergence. The *transitional* demand which flows from the recognition of this historical development, has to be a conscious and collective demand for the abolition of the interest-bearing loans which, by various and often devious means, are loaded onto the international working class through the subservient agency of the nation-state system.

Given the contemporary global situation, a revolutionary movement which struggles to intervene in order to change that situation, can be confident that a *transitional* demand for the abolition of all interest-bearing loans will no longer appear to be a merely utopian wish for an alternative world, entertained by a few individual dreamers. It has become a new necessity confronting the vast majority. In his *Preface to a Critique of Political Economy* Karl Marx made a crucial connection between an objective development and the conscious response to it:

> No social order ever perishes before all the productive forces for which there is room in it have developed; and new, higher relations of production never appear before the material conditions of their existence have matured in the womb of the old society itself. Therefore mankind always sets itself only such tasks as it can solve; since, looking at the matter more closely, it will always be found that *the task itself arises only when the material conditions for its solution already exist or are at least in the process of formation* [emphasis added].[19]

In the current situation, the concept of "the international working class" is not just an abstract idea, or a merely utopian aspiration, because the capitalist system itself has already developed the objective process of uniting the working class through the international integration of the stages of production and chains of distribution. Marx's "old mole" is at work again, undermining the established and apparently stable order.[20] There is a dialectical relationship between this objective process of increasing global unification of the working class and the dissociative nation-states system which sustains the rule of capital by dividing the working class against itself. The ideology of nationalism is not just an expression of the existing system of nation-states. Nationalism is integral to the struggle of *international* capital to prevent the unification of its antagonists (who are the potential grave-diggers of capitalism itself). But, despite the competitive divisions and antagonisms imposed by the nation-states system, the current situation of exploding indebtedness provides the historically new conditions of possibility for uniting the increasing numbers of the global working class *politically*. This conscious internationalism is achievable through the *transitional* demand for the abolition of the increasing debt burdens imposed on the rapidly growing

[19] Karl Marx, *Selected Writings: The 'Economics' 1857–1867*, David McLellan, OUP 1977, p. 390.

[20] Karl Marx, *The Eighteenth Brumaire of Louis Napoleon*. Marx borrows the "Old Mole" from the end of Hegel's *Philosophy of History*, and Hegel borrowed it from Shakespeare's *Hamlet* 1.v to illustrate the dialectic of history concealed beneath the visible stage.

numbers of the exploited by the diminishing number of international super-exploiters. The English poet Shelley's well-known words: "Ye are many, they are few" have never been truer than at the present moment. The "many" have nothing to lose but their debts. However, we can also be certain that the unremitting demand for the repayment of interest on the national debts will come masked in the patriotic language of the need to defend the various fatherlands and motherlands against each other in a rivalry created and financed by international capital. The struggle against nationalist ideology, and the nation-state structure which it supports and justifies, is unavoidable if the market-driven demand for patriotic mutual destruction is to be overcome. There is still a world to win.

Index

The page numbers followed by 'n' represents footnotes.

J. Hall, *The Unfinished History of the Indebted Nation-State*,
https://doi.org/10.1007/978-3-031-84002-9